Understanding business

Teachers' guide to Marketing and production decisions

New edition

Peter Tinniswood

Longman

Understanding Business
Series Editor: Richard Barker
Titles in the Series:
Accounting and financial decisions
Marketing and production decisions
Organizational decision making
Quantitative decision making
Case studies for decision making

Longman Group UK Limited
Longman House
Burnt Mill, Harlow, Essex CM20 2JE, England
and Associated Companies throughout the world

First published 1991

Set in 10/12 Plantin, Linotronic 202

Printed in Great Britain by York Publishing Services

Contents

A note for teachers

This Guide is designed to use with the book *Marketing and production decisions* by Peter Tinniswood. It provides a further understanding of the purpose, design and possible use of the main text; it also offers solutions to most of the questions in the Work sections. It may be of value either to lecturers/teachers or to students studying on their own.

This Guide, like the others in this series, is laid out as follows. The Introduction expands the purpose, level, contents and approach of the book. Thereafter, chapters in the teacher's guide give guidance to the corresponding chapters in the student's text, for example, notes on Chapter 5 in the Students' text are in Chapter 5 in the guide. This guidance includes a further note on the objectives of each chapter and the main teaching points, followed by the 'Guide to exercises' which provides solutions to the Section B questions in the Work section. The implications of these comments might usefully be considered before lessons are planned. Please treat the comments with a pinch of salt for we all have notoriously independent views. There is room within the Guide for you to append additional approaches and ideas for future use.

Our choice of material for this book has been coloured by the presence of four other books in the Series: *Accounting and financial decisions* (Professor D.R. Myddelton), *Organizational decision making* (C. Dearden & M. Foster), *Quantitative decision making* (J. Powell), *Case studies for decision making* (P.M. Tinniswood). You will see that within each book there are a large number of questions. We would expect users to select from these, and other materials, according to the needs of particular examinations.

The Introduction to the series and the Preface, which stand at the front of the Students' text, have not been reproduced here. They should be read to gain an understanding of the purpose and philosophy of the series and to establish the particular teaching methods which are employed throughout these books. We hope that these methods will prove instructive and interesting; we acknowledge that teachers will employ materials as they feel fit; we would welcome comments to help improve further editions of this text.

Richard Barker
Series Editor

Introduction

Marketing and production decisions is a book in the 'Understanding business' series and it looks at marketing and production from a decision-making viewpoint. Marketing and production fit together since each influences the other and acts as a constraint on what can be achieved. Marketing is a very participative element of a business studies course and is best taught through case examples. Students are faced with aspects of marketing every day through advertising and through their purchases of goods and services. They come across design all the time and examination of products can be an instructive way to break into production as an area of study. The book leaves many of the numerate production techniques, such as operations research, critical path analysis and optimum stock ordering quantities, to another title in the series, *Quantitative decision making*, by John Powell. The approach in this book is to develop an understanding of how marketing and production interrelate and the way they influence decision making. Objectives and decisions in one area have an immediate impact on the other.

The decision-making framework is examined in Chapter 2. Although set in a marketing context, the idea of objectives, information and analysis, choice, planning, control and review is as applicable to production.

Level, courses, ages

The primary purpose of this book is to provide material suitable for the theoretical papers and project assignments which are part of Business Studies AS and A-level courses. It is applicable for first-year degree courses and some industry-linked programmes.

Contents

Chapter 1 provides a broad introduction to both marketing and production, looking at the growth of marketing and the change from product-orientation to a greater understanding of the market. There is a brief discussion of the importance of production in terms of wealth creation and the need to match the requirements of the market. Costs are as important as revenue in determining profit and returns on investment. Chapter 2 develops the marketing model and looks at constraints, particularly the economic environment. It is not an examination of economic theory but rather a look at economic issues such as inflation, rates of interest and exchange rates and the way they affect the decisions and practice of marketing and production leading to their impact on profit. Chapter 3 looks at the theoretical nature of demand and the idea of elasticity; this leads to the specific nature of information required to make decisions in Chapter 4. Chapter 5 covers the product and its position within a range of goods and services taking the product life cycle and product portfolio as the basis for analysis and planning. Here a key link with production is introduced through value analysis.

The marketing mix, covered in detail in Chapters 6 to 9, is the basis for tactical marketing decisions. Each aspect of the mix is examined as part of an integrated approach to the market. Chapter 10 introduces different types of production and the way they fit particular strengths and weaknesses of the firm's position in the market. Stock control is treated descriptively. The financial aspects of stock control are examined in another book in this 'Understanding business' series, *Accounting and financial decisions* by David Myddelton. In Chapter 11 work study and quality control are introduced as part of production planning, but they apply to marketing as well in terms of costs and the product that is being provided. Chapter 12 covers control and review as a means of checking performance against objectives and setting new targets for the future. An additional Section D is provided in the Work section with two general case studies.

Approach

The marketing and production areas are continuous. Much of the possible numerate and technique material, such as costing, operations research, and forecasting, is covered elsewhere in the series and can be introduced in more detail where the text refers to it if the teacher wants. There is a danger in breaking up the continuity by constant diversion into techniques, but if they are to be covered then the flow of this text allows numerate work to be broken down into manageable chunks. The marketing mix needs to be introduced early on in the course. Chapter 2 gives a broad overview of the mix and this is useful for the ideas that follow, before greater elaboration later in the book.

Teachers will have their own methods and ideas about dealing with the area. For those new to the series, the Work section at the end of each chapter is divided into three. The Section A questions revise the content of the chapter and consist of short questions. Section B contains short to medium length case studies and exercises which require the student to think about the chapter and apply the ideas in 'practical' situations or practice techniques. Section C provides essay questions that vary from the descriptive to the analytical. The intention is for teachers to make a careful selection of the questions suitable to the group rather than attempt to cover all of them. (Answers to the Section B questions only are given in this guide.)

Sources

Newspapers and periodicals are the best sources of up-to-date case material. *Management Today* and *The Financial Times* are good sources, as are various programmes on television. The business sections of the 'serious' daily and Sunday papers often provide good examples.

There are many useful books covering marketing and production.
Particularly useful are:
Baker, M. J. (1987) *The Marketing Book*. Institute of Marketing.
Davidson, J. H. (1975) *Offensive marketing*. Penguin.
Evans, J. R. and Berman, B. (1987) *Marketing*. Collier Macmillan.
Krajewski, L. J. and Ritzman, L. P. (1987) *Operations management*. Addison-Wesley.
O'Shaughnessy, J. (1984) *Competitive marketing*. A strategic approach. Allen and Unwin.
Pollard, M. (1988) *Advertising*. Penguin.

The answers given to the Examination board questions are the sole responsibility of the author and have not been provided or approved by any Examination board.

1

Introduction to marketing and production

Introduction

This chapter is designed to set the student thinking about marketing and production and to give some indication of the areas covered. It is general and includes some explanation of why marketing has become an essential part of business activity. Some of the ideas, such as economies of scale, link with production and serve to bring the two areas into context together.

For teaching purposes any current examples from the media can be used to expand the ideas. There are no case studies for this chapter.

Main teaching points

1.1 *What are marketing and production?*
Many students will think of marketing in terms of advertising. The key part of this chapter is to introduce them to the wide nature of marketing and its input into production. The idea of market research finding out what consumers want and trying to relate the output of the firm to the demands of the market.

Production covers services as much as goods and this needs to be brought home to students. Many of the production techniques used in mass production of goods can be applied to services. Banks provide a good example of this. Students can develop their ideas on this in discussion.

1.2 *The change from product to market orientation*
Mass production led to the need for marketing to ensure that sufficient sales are made to use the output that mass production creates. Economies of scale: lower unit costs resulting from larger scale of production, that is, more fixed costs through increased capacity spread over the larger output. *Not* fuller use of existing capacity so leading to lower unit fixed costs. Often variable costs per unit will fall as scale increases.

1.3   *The importance of production*
Ideas of value added and wealth creation. There is an opportunity to
discuss the need for tradeables for export earnings to pay for imports.
Invisible imports and exports just as important as visibles.

1.4   *The importance of marketing*
Crucial importance of finding out what the market wants, to avoid wasted
and expensive resource use producing something that the consumer does
not demand. Need to tell the market about products and to distribute
them so that they can be bought by the consumer or firm. Increasing
standard of living in part the result of marketing.

2

The marketing model

Introduction

The chapter provides a framework for the marketing part of the course and is often the first time that students see the decision-making model working over an extended area. The section on constraints looks at the economic environment and can be built on by the teacher. The idea is to show how the economy affects the ability of firms to operate, make decisions and generate profits or surpluses.

Main teaching points

2.2   *The model in detail*

Some time should be spent on this, developing the stages and emphasizing various parts of the model. Objective setting and its importance in giving direction to the marketing function should be stressed. Examples of strategic and tactical objectives and their relationship can be used to give life to the theory. Breadth of objectives should be looked at – image, sales volume and value, market share, market penetration, segments, profit, etc. – and the way objectives influence the tactical decisions of the mix. The setting of objectives must take into account the experience of the firm, its production capacities and skills, and the strengths and weaknesses of the firm. The idea of market niches can be explored.

When looking at the types of information available, some practice at different forms of presenting information (histograms, bar charts, graphs, pie charts, etc.) can be undertaken. There is a danger in believing the accuracy of information, especially when it is numerate. It is important to keep students aware of the qualitative information as well as the quantitative.

The range of choices open to the firm may well be large and needs to be set against limited resources. Diversification, product development and the need to define the market that the firm is in lead to the idea of different market segments. In the 'mix', stress the need to integrate the different aspects and to reflect the type of product/production system/ market to be served.

2.3   Constraints

Key ideas to introduce here include the basic ideas of national income and the way it varies. Students need to understand the language and the way in which the economy can affect the demand for goods and services and the costs of producing them. Always keep in mind the way different aspects affect each other – for example, a rise in the balance of payments deficit leading to a fall in income. For the purposes of the firm, income is particularly important for goods and services whose demand is income elastic. Although elasticity is introduced formally in Chapter 3 it is worth spending a little time on the idea at this stage, showing how exchange rates affect demand through price changes in the international markets. The economic constraints should be looked at in terms of their effects on the firm. Effects on revenue and costs can be linked to profit.

Guide to Exercises

B1   Teachers may find it useful to get groups of three to do this case together and then present findings in terms of the decision-making model. The exercise is largely a comprehension and classification test but it can be enlarged by reference to publications such as *Social Trends* (HMSO) or *The Marketing Pocket Book* published by The Advertising Association. Both these sources contain a mass of statistical information that can be used in many different marketing exercises.

    a.   *Objectives*:
- Long-term profitability.
- Market share of Unilever in washing-powder market.
- Development of new products to meet new market conditions.
- Product objectives:
  cleanliness.
  whiteness.
  flexibility of use in different washing
  cycles/temperatures/fabric types.

    Information and analysis:
- New washing-machine types requiring new powder.
- Low lather.
- Growth of front-loading automatics: 5% in UK, 40% in Italy, 52% in Germany (1970).
- At this stage you can touch on membership of the EC, and the dominance of the Italians in the manufacture of white goods (washing machines and fridges in particular).
- UK ownership up to 88% in 1988.
- Trends in what is happening in other countries (also discuss the growth of liquid detergents for clothes washing in machines).

Alternatives:
- New brand name *v.* use of Persil Automatic.

Action:
- Test market in Yorkshire.
- Difficulty of breaking into distribution channels.
- Poor results.
- Successful second test market in the South East followed by national launch.

  b. Problems with the brand name were:
- *Persil Automatic* – confusion with existing *Persil* name, hence wrong product used for type of machine so leading to less good wash. This would damage Persil image.

  Less flexibility in new product image.
- *Skip* – no help from existing brand both for consumer and distributors. More expensive building up image and consumer awareness of new product.

  c. Test-market failure in the Yorkshire region was the result of difficulty in breaking into distribution channels and also the much lower level of front-loader washing-machine ownership. Thus the demand for the product was not there, whereas higher ownership in the South East meant that the consumer needed the new product. Since many washing machines suggest the product to be used, new owners will look for the powder brand in the shops. The failure was probably not the result of the name. *Skip* is used throughout the continent.

B2 This case is designed to encourage students to think about the way economic conditions affect markets.

  a. *Objectives* – the company has no experience of the DIY market but they do think that they have a better product. They want to 'capture a large slice of the market'. One question is whether this is a realistic objective. A buoyant market means that there may be room for new competitors but this company has no experience of the distribution, etc., required in the consumer market. They need to ensure that they have sufficient production capacity to meet high-volume demand. Have they the experience of high-volume production? A better objective in the first instance might be to 'skim' the market.

  Objectives should be set in terms of volume of sales, market share required, return on investment.

  b. Marketing strategy will depend on the objectives they set. If they go for high volume, selling will need to be done through multiple and DIY buying offices. Promotion will be necessary to persuade distributors to stock the product and to encourage consumers to purchase. The development of the name and capitalizing on performance in the industrial field (bearing in mind that consumers may be very unfamiliar with the name) will be a top priority.

If the company goes for smaller volume, higher price (and therefore higher margins) the strategy will be more restricted: i.e. limited outlets, higher dealer margins, specific promotion in, for example, DIY magazines for the specialist, emphasis on *quality* product. This gives the company the chance to establish itself in the market, learn about the distribution, etc. gear up production and expand and diversify product price and range. It is also a less obvious threat to mass manufacturers in the early stages. Establishing a real quality image should give it a competitive advantage as it expands the market. By avoiding price as the main competitive advantage, demand for the product will be less price sensitive.

c. Control of inflation is likely to be through high rates of interest (monetary policy) or rising taxes (fiscal policy). This could be the moment to discuss some of the economic ideas. Both methods will be disadvantageous to sales and may lead to recession. If they are effective in curbing inflation then the long-term outlook will be better since investment risk will be reduced. There are likely exchange-rate effects resulting from the measures taken to control inflation and their effectiveness.

d. *High rates of interest*:

- Consumers may save rather than spend; particularly damaging for consumer durable like cordless drills since their purchase can be delayed.
- Cost of credit is higher so reducing demand for consumer durables (hire-purchase, bank loans, etc.).
- Cost of holding stocks and advancing credit to customers is higher (debtors).
- Higher rates of interest will tend to cause the value of the pound to rise. This will make imports cheaper and exports more expensive (given certain assumptions about the way companies pass on exchange-rate changes in terms of higher/lower prices) so increasing the competitive pressure on the company. Particularly important if they have decided to compete on price terms in order to achieve the high volume of sales they originally wanted.
- Falling incomes will affect sales if the demand is income elastic (likely for cordless drills).

Higher taxes:

- If indirect taxes are raised (VAT) then prices will rise. Effect on the firm dependent on how price elastic the demand for the drills is.

- If direct taxes are raised (income tax) then income elasticity will be more important; inevitably 'luxuries' like cordless drills will be pushed further down the priorities of consumers. Higher corporation tax reduces the return on investment for the company, hence discouraging further investment.

  Sales revenue will be down, costs up (including finance costs; impact dependent on how highly geared the company is) so profits will fall. Further investment to expand with the market will be in doubt (higher rate of interest means fewer projects yielding positive net present values when discounted at a higher discount rate).

B3   Anticipated sales are 150,000 units for the UK market. The German heating element accounts for 25% of the variable costs, i.e. £15 worth two years ago when the exchange rate was DM4.50 = £1.00.

Thus heating element cost = £15 × DM4.50 = DM67.5.

a.   When exchange rate is £1.00 = $1.80, DM2.60:

			(£ m.)	(£ m.)
Sales	(UK)	150,000 × £100	15.0	
	(US)	150,000 × £100	15.0	30.0
Variable costs				
(domestic)		300,000 × £45	13.5	
(German)		300,000 × £26[1]	7.8	21.3
Contribution				8.7

[1]DM67.50 @ DM2.60 = £1.00 = £26

b.   When exchange rate is £1.00 = $2.00, DM2.70:

			(£ m.)	(£ m.)
Sales	(UK)	150,000 × £100	15.0	
	(US)	135,000 × £100	13.5	28.5
Variable costs				
(domestic)		285,000 × £45	12.8	
(German)		285,000 × £25[2]	7.1	19.9
Contribution				8.6

[2]DM67.50 @ DM2.70 = £1.00 = £25

c. The contribution is very close between these two exchange rates, thus other factors need to be taken into account. If the firm keeps the dollar price at $225 the following situation will occur:

When exchange rate is £1.00 = $1.80, DM2.60:

(£ m.) (£ m.)

Sales	(UK)	150,000 × £100	15.0	
	(US)	125,000 × £125[3]	15.6	30.6

Variable costs			
(domestic)	275,000 × £45	12.4	
(German)	275,000 × £26[4]	7.2	19.6

Contribution	11.0

[3]$225 @ $1.80 = £1.00 = £125
[4]DM67.50 @ DM2.60 = £1.00 = £26

When exchange rate is £1.00 = $2.00, DM2.70:

(£ m.) (£ m.)

Sales	(UK)	150,000 × £100	15.0	
	(US)	125,000 × £112.5[5]	14.1	29.1

Variable costs			
(domestic)	275,000 × £45	12.4	
(German)	275,000 × £25[6]	6.9	19.3

Contribution	9.8

[5]$225 @ $2.00 = £1.00 = £112.50
[6]DM67.50 @ DM2.70 = £1.00 = £25

Thus, leaving the price at $225 generates a higher contribution than altering it with the exchange rate. Given the uncertainty of exchange-rate movements, it would be better to leave the trolley at the higher price. This reduces pressure on capacity so that if there were an unexpected increase in demand from the home market, the company could meet it. Keeping the price constant also reduces confusion in the US and allows more funds for other forms of promotion rather than price.

3

The demand for goods and services

Introduction

This chapter provides an introduction to the theoretical aspects of demand, largely from the economist's point of view. It is important to be clear about the assumptions and the limitation of their value to the practical marketing manager. Nevertheless, the underlying principles are important to show the sorts of variables that have to be considered.

It is probably worth allowing students to think their own way through likely shapes for demand curves before using the chapter. In that way those who are unfamiliar with graphical representation can accustom themselves to it before reading the chapter.

Elasticity is a central concept and time should be taken to develop it fully so that its applications throughout the course (e.g. international trade) can be picked up again.

The supply/demand relationship is not mentioned until Chapter 9 when pricing is covered, but it is probably worth spending a little time on it now, emphasizing the price mechanism and the way theoretical equilibria are reached. This can build on what has been covered in the constraints section of Chapter 2 and the way exchange rates are determined. Mention should be made of the imperfections that occur, both in terms of people not acting rationally and shortage of information.

Main teaching points

3.2 Demand

The idea of demand backed by the ability to pay is important to firms. It is worth making the distinction between effective demand and potential demand. The latter refers to demand that is available if firms can unlock it. Some discussion of promotion could be included here, as could distribution. The idea of priorities in demand and the way firms try to change the perception of their products to alter their position in the order of priorities can be examined. It is worth stressing that very different types of goods and services compete for consumers' purchasing power.

3.3   *The determinants of demand*

It is worth asking students to produce their own list before reading the chapter. Often supply will come up as the major factor and this can be a good time to look at the price mechanism linking supply and demand. They need to see that demand is different from supply and that the former is taken from the consumer's point of view. Availability may lead to a purchase but that may be more significant in terms of a potential market. Price is seen as such an important determinant of demand that it is worth stressing the other factors and the ways of reducing the significance of price by developing, for example, branding.

3.4   *Movements along, and shifts of, the demand curve*

Concentrate on the difference between price and other factors. For example, in the price/demand curve, only price is looked at as a factor affecting demand. The shortcomings of 'static' theory and *ceteris paribus* can be explored.

3.6   *Elasticity of demand*

Elasticity is of crucial importance. There are problems of gathering the information but the sensitivity of demand to any of the factors affecting it is vital for the firm. Once students have the basic idea, it is worth developing it in terms of other elasticities, such as interest elasticity of investment, the impact on demand resulting from changing exchange rates, etc. I have found that students continually get the equation the wrong way up. My last group suggested Queens Park Rangers as being the best way to remember the order for price elasticity of demand! The next section looks at practical applications for elasticity.

Guide to Exercises

B1   Sales   20,000 cans @ 25p increased to
30,000 cans @ 25p.

$$\text{Price elasticity of demand} = \frac{\%\Delta Q}{\%\,\Delta P}$$

$$\%\Delta Q = \frac{10,000}{20,000} \quad \times 100 \quad = 50\%$$

$$\%\Delta P = \frac{5p}{25p} \quad \times 100 \quad = 20\%$$

$$\text{Therefore elasticity} \quad = \frac{50\%}{20\%} \quad = 2.5$$

Notes:
1.   Ignore the negative sign caused by the drop in price.
2.   Elasticity has no units.

3. When calculating percentages, many students make the error of calculating the change on the final price or volume instead of the starting one.

Nothing definite can be said about profit because there is no information on costs. Elasticity merely provides a measure of the way demand (and hence revenue) will change. Since the price elasticity of demand is greater than one, the drop in price will lead to an increase in total revenue (20,000 @ 25p = £5,000; 30,000 @ 20p = £6,000). Profit would increase if variable cost per unit fell or remained constant and fixed costs were spread over a larger number of units of output (i.e. lower FC/unit).

B2 Increase in advertising expenditure $= \dfrac{£10,000}{£50,000} \times 100 = 20\%$

Increase in sales $= 25\%$

Therefore advertising elasticity of demand $= \dfrac{25\%}{20\%} = 1.25$

People using coffee before advertising was increased = 240,000
(Let x = number of people using coffee before advertising increase: therefore $1.25x = 300,000$, therefore $x = 240,000$.)

For advertising this elasticity is high and there is a remarkable increase in sales. This could be the result of advertising an unknown brand in a highly competitive market – possibly local because of the low expenditure. Sales follow as people decide to try the brand. The brand must also be priced in line with the market and other aspects of the mix must be balanced with price. It is worth pointing out that the increase in sales could be the result of many factors other than advertising.

B3 Reducing high stocks of unsold cameras suggests that either the model had not sold well over Christmas, or that the camera has been overtaken by competitor developments, or that a recession has started.

a. For the standard model prices were cut by 10%. Sales rose by 1,500 to 4,500. Thus the starting sales volume was 3,000 units.

Increase in sales $= \dfrac{1,500}{3,000} \times 100 = 50\%$

So price elasticity of demand $= \dfrac{50\%}{10\%} = 5$

b. If the same elasticity of demand applied to the autofocus, then with a fall in price of 10%, sales should rise to 50%.

The question to ask here is whether it is likely that the autofocus would have the same price elasticity of demand as the standard model. It is more likely that its responsiveness to price is much less

11

since it is more of a luxury product. Factors such as the product's image, design and reputation are more likely to have an impact on sales.

c. The forecast fall in demand might be the result of an anticipated recession, perhaps through cyclical movements or through the policies adopted by the government, e.g. high interest rate or taxes.

Sales of cameras are seasonal and the main rush is before the summer holidays. Thus price reductions may have brought the market forward and led to a greater slump in the second half of the year. The effect of the price cuts in the early months of the year on the sales of Snapshop's standard model suggests that the market is very competitive in terms of price. Other camera makers are likely to reduce prices so creating a price war. Other promotional offers might apply such as free films, etc. Overall the profitability of the industry might suffer.

B4   *Product A*: responsive to income but negative elasticity suggesting an 'inferior' good. Very responsive to price indicating substitution between brands or similar products. Promotion has little effect suggesting that brand loyalty is low. Convenience good? Marketing strategy should be price based, probably with point-of-sale emphasis. Impulse buying? Possible product: less expensive brands of jam, margarine, bread, etc.

Product B: little reaction to price, but income is important. Probably a luxury product and since there is a high promotional elasticity, image creation (e.g. packaging) and maintenance could be important. Exclusivity could add value and the marketing strategy would involve high prices and margins. Returns would be used to consolidate the image. Possible product: perfume.

Product C: price, income and promotion seem to have little effect on sales suggesting a necessity. In determining the marketing strategy, the firm would have to keep an eye on competitors and any new developments they may bring out. Profitability will depend more on cost control and efficient production than any marketing expenditure, although distribution will be important so that the product is always available. Otherwise, consumers will choose the competitors' products. Possible product: salt.

B5   a. Reducing the exchange rate makes imports more expensive and exports cheaper provided the importers and exporters alter their prices to reflect the change in exchange rate. If they do not, then sterling profit margins on exports will increase (same foreign currency price) and margins on imports will fall.

If the price elasticity of demand for imports is less than one, the percentage drop in imports will be less than the percentage increase in price. Thus there will only be a small drop in the foreign exchange needed to purchase imports, and more sterling will be sold on the foreign exchange markets to buy the other currencies. If the elasticity is greater than one, there will be a drop in the sales of sterling necessary to buy imports, since there will be a larger proportional fall in demand for imports than increase in price.

If the price elasticity of demand for exports is less than one, there will be a drop in foreign exchange earned by exports. More will be sold but at a lower foreign currency price. If the elasticity is greater than one, there will be an increase in foreign exchange earned.

For a drop in the exchange rate to improve the balance of payments deficit, the sum of the price elasticities of demand for imports and exports must be greater than one. In practice, for most internationally traded products, income elasticity appears to be greater than price elasticity. Hence successive government policies of deflation to correct balance of payments difficulties. The problem with this approach is that subsequent reflation merely causes the balance of payments problem to reappear.

b. If both exports and imports were price elastic, reducing the exchange rate should lead to an increase in activity as domestic firms increase output for export markets and replace imports with domestically produced goods.

The effect on industry will depend on the effect on individual firms and the way in which these combine to alter levels of aggregate demand, income and output (*cf* multiplier).

Imported raw materials and semi-manufactured goods remain a necessary input to domestic output and they will become more expensive so pushing up costs. Since they form only a part of the total cost of the finished good, the impact on final price will be smaller than the percentage increase in cost of the imported parts. This will feed into the economy in higher prices and hence inflation (which will have a negative effect on business confidence). Increased output might hurt profits if decreasing returns to scale existed.

Before passing on the lower exchange rate in price changes, the firm needs to ensure that it has the capacity to meet the demand. It also needs to be clear that a lower price overseas will not harm the image of the product – given the elasticity mentioned in the question, it is probable that competition is on price grounds. Thus British industry will face a generally better demand situation but the effect on individual firms will depend on their nature and the types of market they are in.

B6 a. 2 m. cars at an average price of £7,500
Price falls by £150 and sales increase to 2.2 m.

$$\% \text{ increase in sales} = \frac{200,000}{2,000,000} \times 100 = 10\%$$

$$\text{% drop in price} = \frac{\pounds 150}{\pounds 7,500} \times 100 = 2\%$$

$$\text{Price elasticity of demand} = \frac{10\%}{2\%} = 5$$

b. Total revenue will rise because the elasticity is greater than one.
    Old revenue: 2 m. at £7,500   = £15,000 m.
    New revenue: 2.2 m. at £7,350 = £16,170 m.
        We cannot say what will happen to profits because there is no cost information. If the unit costs remain the same, cutting the price by £150 will cut profits on the 2 m. cars by £300 m. Whether total profit rises depends on the added contribution coming from the additional 200,000 cars sold.

c. Trade union support for the higher elasticity is likely because it will mean more employment and greater security. By keeping the industry going, trade-union bargaining strength may be increased because jobs are protected and required by management. Equally, there might be opportunities for improved productivity which increases job security for those already employed. Overtime and payment by results would increase take-home pay.

d. If the elasticity is 0.5, a drop in price will lead to a fall in revenue.
    New sales:
    Let the change in sales = $x\%$
    % change in price   = 2%

    Therefore $0.5 = \dfrac{x\%}{2\%}$

    so $x = 1\%$.   Sales increase from 2 m. to 2.02 m.

    Old revenue = £15,000 m.
    New revenue = £14,847 m. (fall in revenue of £153 m.)

e. The information given is for the car market as a whole. This is insufficient for the individual car manufacturer who will want to know his current market share and likely increase.
        The price given is an average; what are the implications for cars either cheaper or more expensive? They are unlikely to be equally price elastic. The cheapest cars are likely to sell largely on price whereas the luxury end of the market will not be much affected by price as the cars sell on other factors. There is no cost information and manufacturers may not be able to afford the price cuts.
        A recession means that income will fall and this may have a larger effect on car sales than a price cut. It could help manufacturers of smaller, less expensive cars. The second-hand market may be stronger as fewer people and companies buy new cars. Alternatively,

lower prices for new cars may depress the second-hand car market which can no longer obtain such high prices since new cars are cheaper.

It might be sensible to spend more on other forms of promotion (free servicing, more accessories, etc.) than to cut prices.

As always, the validity and accuracy of the information must be questioned. The difference in the two price elasticities suggested is large and suggests that accuracy may be suspect. Manufacturers need much more specific information to make sensible decisions.

B7 a. Increase in price from 50p to 60p $= \dfrac{10p}{50p} \times 100 = 20\%$

Drop in demand of 100,000 loaves $= \dfrac{100,000}{300,000} \times 100 = 33.3\%$

Elasticity $= \dfrac{33.3\%}{20\%} = 1.67$

b. Although the demand for bread is not elastic, the demand for one brand of bread is. Competition with other suppliers is strong and a price increase from Beresford unmatched by competitors will lead to consumers switching to another baker.

c. Assume that materials, energy and labour are variable costs.

At 50p:	(£)	*At 60p:*	(£)
Sales revenue			
300,000 @ 50p	150,000	200,000 @ 60p	120,000
Variable costs			
Materials & energy	20,000		13,333[1]
Labour	50,000		33,333[2]
Contribution	80,000		73,334
Fixed costs	70,000		70,000
Profit	10,000		3,334

[1] $\dfrac{£20,000}{300,000} \times 200,000 = £13,333$

[2] $\dfrac{£50,000}{300,000} \times 200,000 = £33,333$

Thus increasing the price is not the best option in terms of Beresfords' profits. It also moves the market out of equilibrium for

Beresfords. Demand falls to 200,000 loaves at 60p but the company's supply of loaves would, according to the figures, rise to 400,000 loaves, leaving a surplus of 200,000 loaves.

d. The demand for Beresfords' bread will depend on its quality and consistency. In addition, given the competitive nature of the market, availability is going to be important and distribution will be a key factor in obtaining sales. Better margins for retailers and help with display, etc. will enhance sales. Freshness and comparison with local bakeries' bread will be important.

e. (i)   Variable costs are those that vary with output either directly or semi-directly. Fixed costs do not vary with output in the short term (i.e. up to a given capacity).

(ii) If variable costs rise by 20% then at an output of 300,000 loaves, £70,000 variable costs will rise by £14,000 to £84,000. In this case, profit will fall from £10,000 to a loss of £4,000.

The higher the output, the more significant the 20% rise in variable costs will be as the relative impact will be greater when compared to fixed costs.

(iii) Rising costs push the supply curve to the left, altering the equilibrium price (see figure 3.1).

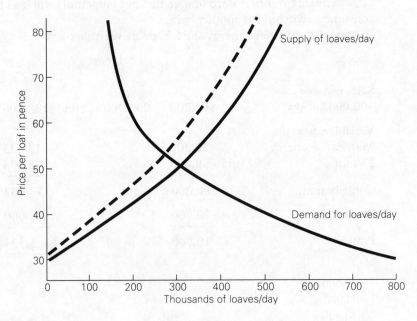

Fig 3.1

B8   a. New sales level when price elasticity of demand is 2:

         Reduction in price   = 10%

         Increase in demand   = 20%

         New sales = 450,000 × 1.2 = 540,000 biros

    b. Old position:

Sales:	450,000 @ 10p	= £45,000
Direct costs:	450,000 @ 5p	= £22,500
Fixed overheads:		= £18,000
	Profit	= £4,500

        (or contribution/biro = 5p

Gross profit = 450,000 × 5p		= £22,500
less overheads		= £18,000
	Profit	= £4,500)

        New position:

Sales:	540,000 @ 9p	= £48,600
Direct costs:	540,000 @ 4.5p	= £24,300
Fixed overheads:		= £23,000
	Profit	= £1,300

So do not increase sales beyond capacity.

    c. New position (2):

Sales:	540,000 @ 9p	= £48,600
Direct costs:	540,000 @ 4.25p	= £22,950
Fixed overheads:		= £21,000
	Profit	= £4,650

    This profit is £150 greater than the previous position. The increase does not justify the investment unless there are further sales expansions expected. Once the company has invested in the new equipment it is more vulnerable if demand falls. Being linked to one supplier could have drawbacks: what will happen to prices next year?

    It may be more sensible to promote sales rather than cut prices and in this way increase contribution and sales.

4

Marketing information

Introduction

This chapter leads on naturally from the previous one. Once the theoretical approach to demand is grasped, its limitations become apparent and the need for specific information on the market is clear. The chapter contains several new ideas, mostly common sense although sadly ignored by many organizations. It might be worth using the greenhouse example as a means of revision. Other examples can be put together easily and exercises can be fun and stimulating. Carrying out some small market-research project either within the school or locally is an instructive way to tackle the area.

There is an appendix at the end of the chapter to introduce some of the statistical techniques and this can be ignored if students want to avoid the numerate area of market research. They are included to show how statistical tools are used in practice. These techniques are examined in more detail in *Quantitative decision making* by John Powell in this series or in any business statistics text.

Main teaching points

4.2 *Market research*
Companies need to find out about their customers, potential customers, competitors and trends in the market. They also need to find out what is happening in allied markets overseas and how general economic conditions are changing in the various markets in which they sell.

4.3 *Types of information*
Stress the various categories of information and the many sources available. The computer through databases has changed the whole approach to information. The danger is that there may be too much and, as always, it is not classified in the way the company wants to use it.

4.4 *Sources of information*
Companies have access to much of their information needs in-house. There are other external sources of data gathered by market research

18

agencies, industry organizations and the government. It is worth showing students a copy of the *Annual Abstract of Statistics* to gain some idea of the sort of information available in published form. Questionnaires are a last resort, since they are expensive and time-consuming to organize. There is more on questionnaire design and sampling (see section 4.7) in *Quantitative decision making (op. cit.)*

4.5   *The specific nature of market research*

The idea of the consumer profile and how it is used is developed here, also the idea of generic needs and specific market segments that must be researched to discover new markets. Constant examination of the market may reveal changes that the company must exploit if it is to increase or maintain market share.

4.6   *Market research and new products*

Most companies survive on developing new products to replace those that are going into decline, so providing a source of future sales revenue. Continuous audits may highlight market changes and competitor advances. Often existing producers may specialize or develop new ideas and market openings may occur for other companies to move in on some of the gaps created. Particular skills or new materials may create new products/markets.

The product map showing the positions of products as they are perceived by consumers and highlighting the possible areas for new products is fun to teach and interests students who can attempt to develop their own product maps.

Guide to Exercises

B1   This case forces students to think about market information and examine it critically.
   a.   Information from secondary sources:
      * Setting up of Post Office sample based on traffic of letters.
      * Sample based on socio-economic groups in the country.
   b.   The Post Office survey is much more favourable. Assuming that the results are not rigged, the differences could be caused by the following:
      * Sample size – Post Office sample reaches more people although it contains fewer letters. What about the 1200 non-returned letters?
      * Sample structure:
         (i) Letter traffic. If more letters (as is likely) are within and between towns the speed of delivery is likely to be higher

than between rural areas. The Post Office survey would have shown this.

(ii) Socio-economic groups. The Users' Council is much more heavily A/B (60%) than the proportion within the population (assuming replies to Post Office Survey reflected actual percentages).

- Collection of information:
  (i) The Post Office knew the date of sending the letters out and could have dispatched them by the earliest post on a slack day. This would increase the chance of a next-day delivery.
  (ii) The Users' Council (pressure group) could have sent their letters by the late post on a Saturday so reducing the number reaching their destination the next day.
  (iii) Selective recall of the letters received by Users' Council. Late letters are most likely to be remembered.
  (iv) Inability to read the postmark leading to a negative rather than a positive date choice; i.e. if in doubt between 9th and 8th as date of posting, the earlier might be chosen.

B2   a.   Sample size $n = 200$

If 70% awareness of *Ozo* then:

Probability that people will know the brand $= p = 0.7$, and
Probability that they will not know the brand $= q = 0.3$
Therefore, mean $= np = 200 \times 0.7 = 140$

$$\sigma = \sqrt{npq} = \sqrt{200 \times 0.7 \times 0.3} \approx 7 \text{ people (6.48)}$$

144 people actually know the brand $= \text{mean} + 4 \text{ people}$

$$4 \text{ people} = \frac{4}{7}\sigma = 0.57\sigma$$

0.57σ is proportional to 22% of the area under the normal curve.
Therefore, there is only 22% certainty that at least 70% awareness exists.

b.   Sample size $n = 1,000$
Mean $= np = 700$ people

$$\sigma = \sqrt{npq} \approx 15 \text{ people}$$

Therefore, to be 99.9% certain ($3 \times \sigma$ to the right of the mean) that there is a 70% awareness, $700 + (3 \times 15) = 745$ people would have to answer favourably. 95.4% confidence would require 730 favourable replies.

c.   As a question, 'With what do you associate the brand name *Ozo*?' is highly unsatisfactory. It is not necessary to have heard the name before to associate something with it. Nor does association necessarily imply the correct one (beef cubes, perhaps?). Thus the findings are useless. They might be of interest if the company were trying to find a name for a new product.

B3

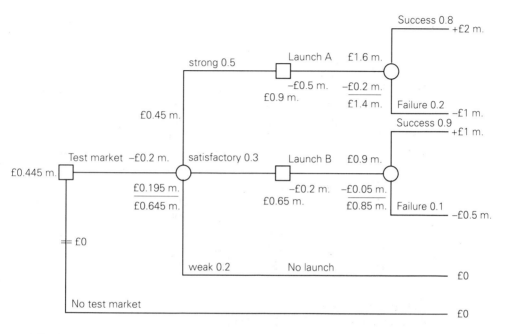

Fig 4.1

On numerate evidence the company should go ahead with test market. However, they must be prepared to risk a loss of £200,000 if the demand is weak, or a maximum loss of £1.75 m. if the demand is strong and Campaign A is used but is a failure. The maximum value of the information is £445,000, since if it costs more it would be cheaper to not employ the test market and do nothing. If the information is not perfect (which it cannot be) its value is less.

B4   a., b.

		Sales index	4-period total	8-period total	Average trend	Seasonal variation	Average seasonal variation
1986	I	95					+6
	II	79					0
	III	88			86	+2	0
	IV	85	347		88	−3	−7
1987	I	91	343	690	91	0	+6
	II	95	359	702	94	+1	0
	III	100	371	730	99	+1	0
	IV	95	381	752	104	−9	−7
1988	I	119	409	790	107	+12	+6
	II	110	424	833	108	+2	0
	III	105	429	853	108	−3	0
	IV	99	433	862	107	−8	−7
1989	I	115	429	862	109	+6	+6
	II	110	429	858	112	−2	0
	III	117	441	870			0
	IV	109	451	892			−7

Likely trend for 1990/I   = 122
Likely trend for 1990/II = 126 (from figure 4.2)

So actual figures = trend plus average seasonal variation
                     1990/I   = 128
                     1990/II = 126

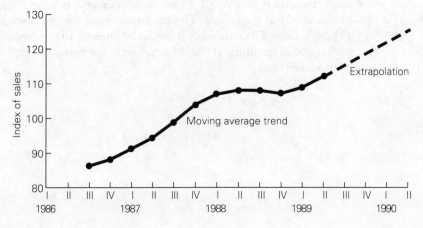

Fig 4.2

It is worth pointing out some of the other factors that might influence the trend. For example, population movements; level of imports; fashion consciousness of market; level of income/state of economy, etc.

Also emphasize the desirability of several forecasts to narrow down the margin of error.

B5 a. Both cluster and quota sampling are cheaper alternatives to random/stratified sampling. Cluster sampling is cheaper than quota since it takes less time and requires less travel but it may give less accurate results. Both are quick ways of gathering information.

    b. The accuracy of the findings is proportional to $1/\sqrt{n}$ where n is the size of the sample. Provided the population is sufficiently large, equal sample sizes should be taken.

    c. Any of cost, time available for the work, population size, accuracy required would limit the size of the sample. Time is crucial because information goes out of date and its value may not be worth the extra cost of a long survey.

    d.

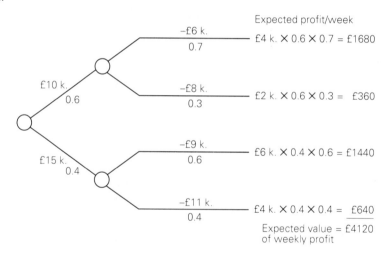

Fig 4.3

B6 The first part of this question should make students think about the way questionnaires are compiled and what is necessary to achieve responses from those asked. The second part looks at ways of displaying the data from questionnaires and how they may be interpreted. This question can be extended to look at pie charts, etc., and give practice in drawing and using them.

    a. The reasons for the questionnaire should be stated and the questions should be straightforward and unambiguous. Jargon should be avoided. There should be no 'leading' questions, no calculation for the respondent, no offensive questions. The questions should ask for answers in units that people use, and where analysis requires specialist information it should be deduced from the answers given. (e.g. if the librarian wanted to find out the ISBNs of the most borrowed books, or which items classified according to the Dewey system were taken out, then the question he would ask would be to find out the titles of the books borrowed. When he was classifying the results of the questionnaire, he could find out the relevant numbers himself.)

The questionnaire should be kept as short as possible and the layout clear both for the respondent to answer and the librarian to collate the information. Where respondents are asked, for example, to explain their reasons, there should be sufficient but not too much space.

b.   (i)

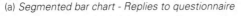

(a) *Segmented bar chart - Replies to questionnaire*

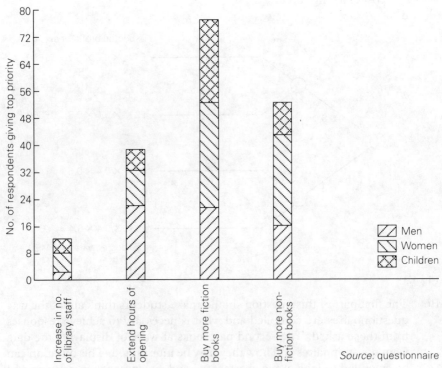

Fig 4.4 (a)

24

(b) *Parallel bar chart - Replies to questionnaire*

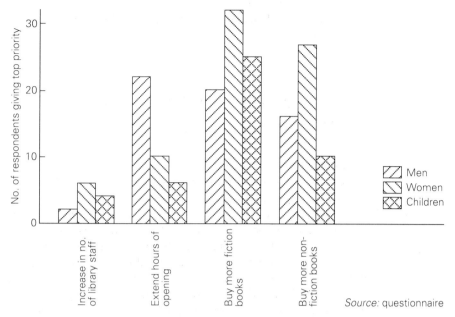

Fig 4.4 (b)

(ii) The segmented bar chart shows the totals clearly but is not so easy for comparison for each division. The parallel bar chart is clearer for each division but less clear for the totals.

(iii) A histogram is a frequency diagram with the area of each rectangle proportional to the magnitude of the variable, not height as with the bar chart. The horizontal axis is a continuous and scaled axis. Bars touch each other if the variable has more than zero frequency. Bars can be of unequal width although this makes interpretation more difficult.

c. (i) Sample size $= 100$ people ($= n$)

If the results were random then $p = 0.5$ and $q = 0.5$ where p is the likelihood of being satisfied and q the likelihood of being dissatisfied.

Mean $= np = 50$ people

$$\sigma = \sqrt{npq} = 5 \text{ people}$$

60% said they were satisfied with the service. This is

$$\frac{60 - 50}{5} = 2\sigma \text{ from the mean}$$

Thus there is confidence at the 95% level but not at the 99% level (three σs from the mean).

(ii) Sample size = 200 people (= n)
If the results were random then p = 0.5 and q = 0.5 where p is the likelihood of being satisfied and q the likelihood of being dissatisfied.
Mean = np = 100 people

$$\sigma = \sqrt{npq} = 7.07$$

60% said they were satisfied with the service. This is

$$\frac{120 - 100}{7.07} = 2.83\sigma \text{ from the mean}$$

Thus there is confidence at the 99% level.

(iii) The principal assumption is that the sample is truly reflective of the whole population and that the answers are honest.

d. The questionnaire could be given to library users when they enter or leave the library, or to people in the street, or as an interview.

The decision between these methods will depend on cost, response rates, interview bias, time available for respondents to answer, the choice of sample (e.g. if it is handed to people *in* the library, the sample already only looks at users and ignores those who might use the library if the service were better). Similarly, response rates might be higher with an interview since a personal approach might result in more replies. However, there is the danger of bias and a greater chance of the respondent giving the answer he/she thinks the interviewer wants.

5

Product policy and planning

Introduction

This chapter introduces the building blocks for product development and planning through the product life cycle and product portfolio matrix. The marketing mix and the factors that influence it are covered in general terms: the following chapters look at each aspect in detail. Value analysis is an important part of product development and continuous evaluation of existing products. It acts as a link between marketing and production as well as ensuring that the best advantage is made of any product that is on the market. Product portfolio analysis and the product life cycle are useful to teach the need to plan and set strategy but their theoretical limitations need stressing. Both are used widely in large companies to determine the future path of product development and the way existing goods and services should be marketed.

Main teaching points

5.1 *The marketing mix*

The first section introduces the elements of the mix and the importance of the relationship between the different aspects to achieve a coherent plan to market goods and services. Choice is constrained by the way the company operates and its strengths and weaknesses. The mix is crucial to achieve the desired product positioning and to match the market segment.

5.2 *Factors affecting the mix*

This section looks at the general factors that influence the mix decisions. They are applicable to each element of the mix. It is worth taking some time over this part since the subsequent chapters are more valuable against this general background.

5.3 *The product*

The main idea to get across is what is meant by a product: stress the different views of suppliers and consumers in terms of the purpose of the product and the way it is used. (Kleenex, for example, introduced facial tissues for removing make-up; they had not seen the potential of the product as a paper handkerchief although that was the way they were used by consumers. Designs were added on paper towels as they came to be used as napkins.)

5.4   *Value analysis*
This section is an important link between production and the market in terms of what is made, how a product is designed for its final use, ease of maintenance and ease of production. These decisions are taken against a background of cost reduction and 'value for money' for the consumer. Successful value analysis in a company can give it a distinct advantage over competitors but for it to work it must have the public and active support and involvement of the top management.

5.5/7 *Product policy*
The key idea here is the importance of managing products and determining the 'distinctive competence' of a company. There are plenty of examples – consulting for small firms, private client stockbroking (an example of a market niche opening up in the light of 'Big Bang'), mass marketing skills, low-cost manufacture, etc. In spite of the work that goes into achieving success, many new products fail.

5.8   *Product portfolio analysis*
One of the two principal ways of analysing a company's position in terms of its product range and where it stands in the market and compared to the competition. It develops the idea of both market share and market growth, and the importance of generating the cash from mature products and markets to finance entry into new markets and new products.

5.9   *The product life cycle*
Important both for explaining and planning market strategy over the life of the product. There are dangers in following it too slavishly in its practical application without reacting to changes in the market. Cycle lengths vary and false alarms of decline can lead to a potentially successful product with future sales being axed. Stress the need to obtain a balance amongst products having some at each stage in the cycle. Real difficulties can be experienced when it comes to removing products from the range.

5.10 *Entrance and exit strategies*
Different approaches to markets according to the strengths and weaknesses of the firm. There can be significant problems resulting from going outside the experience of the firm in terms of scale of production or marketing effort.

Guide to Exercises

B1   a.   Initially, the industry was small facing a limited business market and producing expensive, bulky machines.

New technology, the microchip, enabled smaller machines to be produced at lower prices as volume sales and production reduced unit costs. The chip manufacturers were first in the market but the growth of sales resulted in a large number of other companies coming into the market. As the market matured, so competition intensified and only a small number of large suppliers survived.

(This pattern is a classic example of how an industry changes as products mature: the same is happening in the personal computer industry and, over a much longer time span, in the motor industry.)

b.   *Development*: The first calculator was a business machine with a limited market (Anita: it was labour intensive and the market came to be dominated by the Japanese because of cheap labour in the early 1960s). The product life cycle for the hand-held calculator started with the silicon chip (the development of which was an outcome of research by NASA and thus financed by them). Sinclair was the first company to see the potential of the domestic market and break into it. Texas Instruments was also in at the early stages.

Growth: Once the market potential was realized, the major electronic companies joined in (Casio, Sharp, Toshiba) and the market grew very rapidly. Smaller companies also became involved, many of them assembling components in the Far East. Economies of scale as volume and capacity increased enlarged the market for the product. Vital to the success of the market enlargement was the development of new outlets in the high street. Distribution through the multiples, such as Boots, Laskys, Dixons, gave the market coverage to obtain volume sales.

Maturity: Intensive competition and price cuts signal the mature stage of the cycle. At the same time, new models with very short cycles appear to keep sales up.

Extension strategies: • new uses (LCD display), e.g. watches
• new models and new/more functions
• 'designer' calculators (very slim, etc.)

Problems emerge for distributors and manufacturers with short cycles and lead times. The consequence is fear of being left with stocks of last year's models, insufficient time to test new products, expensive set-up times for the manufacturers.

Intensifying competition where volume is essential both to cut costs of production and to gain massive coverage of retail outlets means that smaller firms are driven out of the market. Lower margins mean that bankruptcy occurs and only tightly cost-controlled companies can remain. To ensure volume as the market growth slows, market share becomes increasingly important.

29

With fewer companies in the market, the number of new models falls and prices become stable. New products using the same technology provide areas of expansion (language dictionaries, spelling machines). Segmentation of the market occurs into, for example, school, university, business. (Hewlett Packard has made the expensive business segment its own.)

The overall demand is that of a mature market, with no decline in evidence.

c. Change from the office equipment to mass market meant development of mass advertising (colour supplements, etc.); advertising concentrating on different facilities of different models, etc.; incentive selling, off-the-page selling, low pricing, wide distribution using mail order and high street stores.

In maturity, the margins have stabilized to give dealers a reasonable return and encourage a willingness to stock the products. Advertising is much reduced as the market is stable.

B2 a. Cadbury's major problem was to find a new product that would appeal to consumers. (Most successful confectionary products are of long standing, *cf* Nestlé's takeover of Rowntree to gain brands and distribution or Cadbury's purchase of Trebor and Bassett.) Cadbury had suffered when Rowntree launched Yorkie and took part of their market for milk chocolate bars.

Aero (a Rowntree product) represented a product type that had potential and did not exist in the Cadbury range.

The test market was linked to production capacity in the new Bournville plant – designed to provide for 20% of the expected national market. The marketing emphasis was on the new taste of the aerated chocolate bar. Tyne Tees was used for the test market because it was a good reflection of the rest of the country – a sort of 'cluster' sample.

Cadbury faced a problem of keeping the product to the region. The 'secrecy' around the new product created its own mystique and the development of a 'black market' provoked interest elsewhere. The launch became a media event and the consequence was that production capacity was insufficient. Cadbury reacted by closing down production and building a new full-scale launch production facility for the re-launch two years later.

b. During the time that Cadbury closed down production, Rowntree introduced a chunky Aero bar – clear example of a 'me-too' product. This could have been a serious problem if they had taken the market from Cadbury; in practice, it did not have a major advertising launch but kept the idea of a chunky aerated chocolate bar alive.

Re-launch options were to go for a national launch or start with a limited launch in one area. If the latter were taken, then the choice of area had to be made. Cadbury decided to use Tyne Tees again and went for a major launch with heavy advertising and promotion. T-shirts, mugs, badges, etc., were used to create interest and the blitz effect of 'Wispamania' built the market up very quickly. National launch followed the Tyne Tees introduction, product extension followed with small bars sold in packs and sales reached £80m. within two years.

B3   This exercise is fun and encourages students to look at products. It can be done with any product where there are different brands and varieties of construction. Points to look for are ease of assembly, number of parts, complexity of each part, materials used, effectiveness of operation, likely areas of breakage or loss (e.g. biro caps), overall aesthetic design. Why do people pay a great deal for expensive ball-points when cheap ones do the same job?

If you take a BIC apart, nothing is screwed in, so doing away with the process of moulding or milling a screw in the material. Everything is push fit, only the tip of the ball is metal, all the rest is plastic. The number of parts is small. Note that the caps have holes in them, introduced some years ago to avoid suffocation if the cap was swallowed.

Parker uses a metal refill with a serrated top to rotate the refill each time it is 'extended', so reducing ball wear. Papermate introduced a pump action to obtain evenness of flow.

The same exercise could be carried out easily with electric plugs, folders, etc.

B4   a.   The speed device sold to police forces has limited outlets. It is a relatively hi-tech product and although it has a significant market share, market growth may not be that large. Any market growth that comes results from decisions by the police authorities. Profits are good but payment may be slow and that may create problems of cash flow for the company. However, the product is a 'cash cow' and should generate cash to be used to help new products and continue product research to keep the police model fully up-to-date, matching any competitive developments. Research and development is important for the company – its distinctive competence.

b.   The new product relies on the company's knowledge of their speed detector provided to the police. Market growth is expected to be large, initial market share is presumably high, thus the product can be categorized as a 'star'. To achieve the cash-cow status, funding will be necessary both to market the product and increase production.

The company does not have the capacity to increase production much on its own site, nor is there the land to expand around the factory. Profits are insufficient to finance the expansion internally. Thus Tustow can try to raise the money through loans, etc. (but gearing problems?) or, if it is large enough, try for a listing on the

31

USM (but control problems and the danger of the market requiring short-term gains; particularly a problem for a company relying on research and development and long-term strategies).

Tustow has no experience in either mass production or mass marketing. There is a danger that expansion into this area will use up all funds and starve the R & D necessary for it to develop other products in its traditional area. It might be better to license manufacture and sales to another larger company with more experience in this area. The danger here is that me-too products might emerge.

B5   *Table showing the sales volume, value and profits for each product.*

Product 1

Year	Quantity (units)	Price/ unit (£)	Sales value (£)	Profit (£)	Rev.* % of	Profit+ total
19 × 1	2,100	12	25200	3150	21.9	13.4
19 × 2	2,500	15	37500	4687.5	28.2	17.4
19 × 3	2,800	20	56000	7000	31.7	20.0
19 × 4	2,800	24	67200	8400	33.4	21.1
19 × 5	2,900	29	84100	10512.5	36.7	23.0
19 × 6	3,100	30	93000	11625	39.8	24.8

Product 2

Year	Quantity (units)	Price/ unit (£)	Sales value (£)	Profit (£)	Rev.* % of	Profit+ total
19 × 1	3,000	8	24000	7200	20.8	30.6
19 × 2	3,200	10	32000	9600	24.0	35.5
19 × 3	3,300	12	39600	11880	22.4	33.9
19 × 4	3,300	14	46200	13860	22.9	34.8
19 × 5	3,400	18	61200	18360	26.7	40.2
19 × 6	3,200	22	70400	21120	30.1	45.1

Product 3

Year	Quantity (units)	Price/ unit (£)	Sales value (£)	Profit (£)	Rev.* % of	Profit+ total
19 × 1	6,000	11	66000	13200	57.3	56.1
19 × 2	5,300	12	63600	12720	47.8	47.1
19 × 3	4,500	18	81000	16200	45.9	46.2
19 × 4	4,400	20	88000	17600	43.7	44.2
19 × 5	4,200	20	84000	16800	36.6	36.8
19 × 6	3,700	19	70300	14060	30.0	30.0

| | | All products | |
Year	Total units	Total sales (£)	Total profit (£)
19 × 1	11100	115200	23550
19 × 2	11000	133100	27007.5
19 × 3	10600	176600	35080
19 × 4	10500	201400	39860
19 × 5	10500	229300	45672.5
19 × 6	10000	233700	46805

* Rev % of is the percentage of total revenue for the year provided by the product.

\+ Profit as a percentage of the total profit for the year provided by the product

Note: totals mask movements in each product. The number of units is of little use since prices are different for each product and we are given no information about the production requirements for each.

Product 1 is growing in terms of sales, sales revenue and profit, both in actual terms and as a percentage of totals. Price increases have been sharp and the market has continued to grow.

There is a slight fall off in sales of product 2 in 19×6, but not enough to suggest decline. This product looks mature (in production for 11 years) but its contribution to total profit is rising.

Product 3 profits are falling as a percentage of the total annual profit. Sales are falling suggesting some decline, although the price rise in 19×4 raises revenue for that year. Product 3 continues to provide a larger contribution to profit than product 1. In 19×6 the price has been reduced but sales continue to fall.

Before any decisions on the products can be taken, we need to know whether the economic climate has changed, how each product responds to the level of income, what other products there may be in the pipeline and whether sales of each product are affected by the existence of a range of products A, B and C.

6

Distribution

Introduction

This chapter is the first of four looking at the mix in detail. The treatment is qualitative (transportation techniques appear in *Quantitative decision making* in this series). Central ideas include the objectives of the company in terms of product control, cost, expertise, quality and the willingness/ability to push one manufacturer's brand versus another. The functions of the middleman and the value of the services provided are compared with the opportunity cost of doing without wholesalers and retailers.

Main teaching points

6.2 *Objectives in distribution*
     The objective of any distribution system is to get products to the right place at the right time in the right condition, consistent with costs and other objectives of the company – market share, coverage, etc.

6.3 *Types of distribution channel*
     Examples of different distribution channels are given in this section. It is worth discussing with students the 'best' channel to suit different requirements.

6.4 *Middlemen*
     Middlemen provide a service that has to be paid for through dealer mark-ups. The supplier must decide whether the service provided by dealers is worth the cost involved. Knowledge of the market, bulk-breaking and stockholding are the three most important services provided. Knowledge of the market may be vital for a company that is new to that market or that does not know it well. Middlemen provide the contacts and experience of the markets. Bulk-breaking concerns cost reduction by providing a distribution service in small quantities for several suppliers.

Stockholding reduces the working capital needs of the supplier by taking stocks and generating cash for the supplier before the goods are sold to the final consumer. Some of the *risk* of selling is reduced for the supplier although the failure of a product may make it more difficult to persuade a middleman to take on new products from the same supplier.

Types of middlemen include wholesalers and retailers. The more links in the distribution chain, the greater are the costs and the more inflexible the pricing structure, since increases at factory level lead to constant percentage mark-ups through the chain. If a long chain is used, goods are handled more and there are more costs involved; there is a greater risk of obsolescence and damage.

6.5   *Direct selling*
Distribution through this method may be the correct solution for certain types of goods. Sophisticated technology and complex industrial goods may be sold direct and made to order. Where the link between the supplier and purchaser has to be close or where goods are perishable there is a case for direct selling although the value of the product needs to be high to justify it.

6.6   *Competition in the distribution channel*
This section looks at the types of competition that exist between distributors for a particular supplier's product and competition between two or more suppliers to ensure that distribution gives them the best deal in terms of exposure and selling.

6.7   *Control of the distribution channel*
The balance of power between distributors and suppliers will, in part, determine the distribution channel chosen. As retailers have grown in size and their purchasing power has increased, the position of the manufacturer has been down-graded. The relative importance of the wholesaler is under pressure in high-volume transactions. Competition forces middlemen to consider their contribution to the distribution process.

6.8   *The choice of distribution channel*
The choice of channel is dependent on the nature of the market, the type of product, the nature of the company, the type of middleman and the market coverage required by the manufacturer. Once a distribution channel has been set up there is often a reluctance to change because of the loyalties and relationships built up. These take time and goodwill and may be more important than temporary better deals provided by competitors.

Guide to Exercises

B1 This question is designed to get the student to think about distribution channels and is probably useful for discussion. There are no definite answers.

  a. Bottled beer
   ● Branded consumer good.
   ● Maintenance of quality important but largely covered by packaging.
   ● Low value and long lasting so could be long chain (little cash tied up in stocks).
   ● Supermarkets and small stores (including specialist wine shops) and pubs.

  So distribution must be wide – go via wholesaler? *or* for bulk purchase, e.g. by supermarkets, deliver direct from manufacturer.

  b. Radio alarm clock
   ● Sell through retailer but competition is severe so keep channel as short as possible (pricing implications).
   ● High value to weight and volume – direct mail order.
   ● Discount stores important; again sell direct.

  c. Fresh vegetables
   ● As direct as possible to keep vegetables fresh.
   ● Some from farms sold direct to customers (farm shops) and local retailers.
   ● Wholesaling function, e.g. Covent Garden to distribute to town outlets.

  d. Household furniture
   ● Chain stores receive direct from manufacturer (reduce costs, large orders – compare MFI with huge sales of home assembled furniture).
   ● Specialist and expensive furniture wholesale with retailers providing delivery and in some cases installation. Importance of image.

  e. Complex piece of industrial pumping gear
   ● Direct sale to few industrial users.
   ● Installation and explanation carried out by manufacturer.
   ● Reduce number of people involved in technical complexities.

B2   Distribution channel:

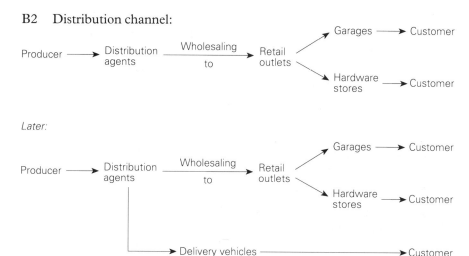

Fig 6.1

Poor sales because:
(i)   Delivery might make the cost to customer greater.
(ii) Self-service garages made customers handle the product.
(iii) Heavy to carry.
(iv) Shortage of space in hardware stores (Health and Safety?).
(v)   Market more concerned with convenience of heating – central heating?

B3   a. Handiman's price is higher because it has to finance the wholesaling function – stockholding, distribution to retailers, etc.
     b. Final price for Hobbihouse:
         = £1.20 ex-factory
       + 15% = £1.38 (wholesaler margin)
       + 33% = £1.84 (retailer margin)
       Final price = £1.84 per pack

       Final price for Handiman:
         = £1.30 ex-factory
       + 33% = £1.73 (retailer margin)
       Final price = £1.73 per pack.
     c. There is no clear answer on the information given but:
         (i)   Firms are new to the market and so have no knowledge of the market or distribution methods.
         (ii) Handiman have decided to sell straight to retailers and with no prior reputation it may be difficult to get them to stock the new product.
         (iii) Once the wholesaler (who has good contacts) has established a new brand, retailers will be reluctant to accept yet another.
         (iv) But – Handiman does have a price advantage over Hobbihouse.

So Handiman is choosing a course where the risk is high since the chances of breaking into the market are small. If they succeed, then the price advantage will work in their favour. On balance, given the importance of the wholesaler in the local area, Hobbihouse is probably pursuing the best course of action.

B4   Advantages of leaving selling to wholesaler:
●   Fewer visits.
●   Freedom for wholesaler (success of product will determine his emphasis).
●   Lower selling costs.
●   Smaller sales force.

Disadvantages of leaving selling to wholesaler:
●   He may not push the product.
●   Only part of the whole range sold by wholesaler so it receives less attention.
●   Problems of servicing equipment for maintenance.
●   Mark-up: need to match competitor's incentives.

Direct selling – emphasis on product – real sales pressure:
●   Clear knowledge of retailer's views.
●   Greater ability to provide technical service and repairs.
●   Cuts out wholesaler mark-up.
●   But could be expensive with more people involved.
    In this case it may be better to leave selling to the wholesaler and rely on good press reviews and advertising to create demand for the amplifier. If the company has any large customers then it could sell direct to them but it is unlikely to have a large sales force. Small size of company implies that output will not be very high so it should choose specialist outlets – 'franchises' – to cover maintenance.

B5   Total relevant market for paint = 1.4 million cars (although how many of these are office cars and therefore unlikely to be repaired at home?). Probably use wholesalers because of wide market although sell direct to the buying agents of the national chains.
    Possibly the garage outlets will have central buying agencies by ownership (e.g. major oil companies).
    Figure 6.2 shows a probable distribution chain:

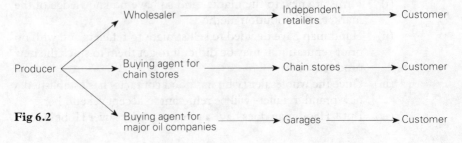

Fig 6.2

7

Advertising

Introduction

Advertising is the high profile area of marketing and the temptation to talk only about advertisements must be resisted. The chapter looks at the broad structure of advertising and its process. There are plenty of current examples to look at and discussion of the ideas and the way advertisements attempt to persuade and develop product images can be valuable. If you can persuade someone from an advertising agency to come down and talk to students the impact is considerable, particularly if they bring some advertisements with them. The best structure for such a talk is to start with the product idea and work through to the final advertisement, situating this in the overall mix.

Advertising ties in with communication and perception and it can be a useful preview or review of the human area depending on the relative position of marketing and the human area in the course.

Main teaching points

7.2   *The range of advertising*
Many students think of advertising in terms of television. It is important to outline the breadth of advertising not only through the variety of media used, the emphasis on consumer goods and the persuasive side of the subject, but also as a means of disseminating information by, for example, the government, classified advertising for goods wanted or for sale, situations vacant, etc.

7.3   *Advertising and the mix*
Advertising is part of the mix and the selling effort. Point out the links between advertising and, for example, package design, where advertisements pick out the pack so that consumers will notice it in shelf displays in shops. Advertising should reflect the image and distinctiveness that the company wants to portray.

7.4   *The structure of advertising*
This section looks at the relationship between the advertiser, agencies and

media. The objective of advertising is to create awareness and generate positive feelings towards the product.

Product ➤ Filters ➤ Perceived product

- attitudes
- experience
- information
- image
- advertising

Agencies provide creative work and, with media agencies where they are separate, buy space to position advertisements. Some time should be spent on the relative costs of media and the appropriateness for the product and the budget available.

7.5   *The advertising decision*
It is often difficult to measure the effectiveness of advertising but companies need to set objectives and measure results against them. Response rates and sales volume can be monitored and give some idea of how effective the advertising and promotion is. As with other parts of the mix, some of the change may be the result of non-advertising factors such as the actions of competitors or changes in the way goods are displayed, etc.

Expenditure on advertising and setting a realistic budget can be done in several ways. It is a hit and miss affair with agencies often advocating more expenditure than a company wants. Some of the decision will depend on the profitability of the company and the position of the product in its life cycle as well as what competitors are doing. Economic factors such as the level of income are important as well.

7.6   *Controls on advertising*
The advertising industry has controls to prevent malpractice and to try to ensure that advertising is not misleading or offensive. Some discussion of the importance of controls is useful, developing the idea of self-regulation and the reputation of an industry.

Guide to Exercises

B1   Cost per 1,000 circulation:

Today $\dfrac{£24}{597,000}$ ×   1,000   =   £0.040

Daily Telegraph $\dfrac{£61.50}{1,107,000}$ ×   1,000   =   £0.056

Not asked for, but of interest, is the cost per 1,000 readers:

Today $\dfrac{£0.040}{2.6 \text{ (readers/copy)}}$ $= £0.0155$

Daily Telegraph $\dfrac{£0.056}{2.5 \text{ (readers/copy)}}$ $= £0.0224$

The choice of paper to use for advertising is only partly dependent on cost. The advertiser must look at the readership profile to ensure that he is reaching the target audience. There is no point in placing an advertisement if it does not reach potential consumers.

The readership profile of the two papers is:

	Sex		*Age group*			*Socio-group*	
	Men	*Women*	*15/34*	*35/54*	*55+*	*ABC_1*	*C_2DE*
	%	%	%	%	%	%	%
Today	56	44	50	32	17	47	54
Daily Telegraph	55	45	25	32	42	79	21

Thus there is little difference in the distribution between men and women for the two papers, but the *Daily Telegraph* is read by a much older group than *Today*. The socio-economic group is also much more heavily weighted to ABC_1 and these two taken together mean that the readers of the *Daily Telegraph* are wealthier and have more disposable income. This information is important for advertisers and much more significant than the cost difference between the two papers for each column inch bought.

B2	*ABC Circulation*	*Readers per copy*	*Readers*
Country Life	55,000	9.4	517,000
Exchange & Mart	69,000	22.6	1,559,400

Exchange & Mart sells 25% more copies but has 3 times as many readers because the readership per copy is so high. Readership of *Exchange & Mart* is predominantly male while *Country Life* has the bulk of its readership from the ABC_1 group.

When deciding on what publication to use to advertise double glazing, the firm will have to find out about its consumer profile. In particular, is the 'buy' decision taken by men or women, what socio-economic group makes up most of the market? The *Radio Times* has a readership of 8.96 m. (3.2 m × 2.8 readers per copy). The attractiveness of each publication will depend on the cost per page of advertising space and its 'fit' with the market. In addition, different publications will carry greater weight for the advertiser depending on the image of the magazine. (Page rates – July 1989 – were: *Country Life*: £1,520, *Exchange & Mart*: £2,616, *Radio Times*: £12,650).

B3   Mustard is a difficult product to advertise. The emphasis needs to be on prominence, to attract consumers' attention and remind them of the product. It was always said that Colman's profit came from the mustard left on people's plates. Increased use may come from frequent commercials and also from new uses (e.g. in sauces) that could be highlighted in advertising. However, low volume of sales means that the advertising budget may not be that large. High street posters might be effective in that they operate at the time customers are buying food products and are not too expensive.

The problem for American mustard is that its packaging is similar to other stronger mustards. Because American mustard is more of a 'relish' and is used in greater quantities, it actually stands out as a major opportunity. Packaging should be different from other mustards and the size of the pack should be larger. Mustard ketchups and opportunities for selling for barbecues should be exploited. The company could also try to increase sales by doing special deals with hamburger chains which would get the product known.

The increase in imports means that the company will have to examine its varieties to ensure that it can match the range of imports. Advertising, emphasizing both the range and the name, should have some impact. Advertising seems to be important since sales fell back by 2% during a break in promotion.

B4   a.   The company is selling personal service and local repair. This is its distinctive competence and sets it apart from large chains selling through cut-price but impersonal stores. As the cut-price stores increase their service the company will find itself under greater pressure. Their emphasis with customers must be on the advice side at the time of purchase.

b.   The store is a local one so advertising must be in the local press, entries in local directories and in free newspapers in the area; Yellow Pages would be another possible place.

Theme of advertising would stress service and also any other promotions that might be used, e.g. free batteries, discounts for customers who produce the advertisement, home delivery and installation (particularly important for those who cannot set up systems), credit.

c.   If the firm does decide to advertise, it would be useful to know something about the pattern of sales (past sales records should provide this). If they are seasonal, then advertising at the start of the season (e.g. autumn up to Christmas) should help to entice sales from the multiples.

d. Comparisons would be made with the previous comparable period. A record of sales, requests for information, number of customers in the store, etc., will give an indication of whether the promotion has been successful. Asking new customers how they heard of the store might also provide useful information.

B5   The chart shows that advertising helps to reduce the price of products. For the advertiser it is a justification for advertising and shows that it can pay for itself through increased sales. For the consumer, by keeping prices down, advertising works in his favour.

These advantages presumably result from volume sales and economies of scale, as well as competitive pressure which keeps prices down. With a higher turnover of products the trade can sell more and so accept lower margins. Advertising is an important factor in deciding to stock products.

Advertising may also have benefited the consumer by informing the market of new or modified products.

But points to notice:

1. Were there any specific conditions that affected the choice of the base period? Manipulation of the base period can influence the apparent results and conclusions.

2. What are the heavily advertised brands and do they reflect the whole food market? Have others suffered as a consequence of the advertising of these brands? Nothing is said about the quality of the food.

3. Is fresh food (i.e. not branded) likely to fluctuate more in price as conditions change?

4. Should the lines really be straight?

8

Sales policy and sales promotion

Introduction

The selling side of the mix relies on the 'push' aspect of getting the product through the distribution channels to the consumer. Sections 8.1 and 8.2 look at the way the sales force can be deployed and the rest of the chapter covers the different aspects of promotion that influence the sales of a product. Branding and packaging are important both for consumer loyalty and product recognition. They are as important in service industries where, for example, a restaurant or hotel chain has a particular image or a bank supplies its documentation and cheque books in a particular format and design.

Sponsorship and public relations are important and increasingly used to help gain a reputation for a company and its products. There are plenty of examples to choose from, with sponsorship being much in evidence in the sports world.

Main teaching points

8.1 *Introduction*
Advertising pulls the consumer to the product while selling pushes the product through the distribution channels to the consumer.

8.2 *The importance of selling*
The sales force is often the only point of contact between outlets and the supplier, especially for small outlets. This can be the main form of communication between the supplier and the customer and from the customer to the supplier. The sales force can help the retailer with the way to display merchandise and how to emphasize its good points.

8.3 *Organization of the selling effort*
This section covers target setting and managing the sales force, taking into account factors relevant to the market or region being covered and the remuneration given to the sales force.

8.4   Sales promotion

Point-of-sale promotion is used to increase product usage, the number of outlets handling the product, raising stock levels and gaining new users.

8.5   Types of sales promotion

Branding has increased customer loyalty as its main aim, so reducing (for example) price competition and the reliance on the marketing mixes of other companies. Packaging protects and provides information and easy recognition for products. Price reductions and special offers are used to increase sales in the short term. Credit policy (debtors) is a well used method of attracting sales for consumer durables and industrial products. The final part of sales promotion lies in the trade fairs and exhibitions where producers and buyers (at whatever level) meet and trade.

Guide to Exercises

B1   Advantage of geographical division:
- Less travelling and so more time to carry out calls.
- Possibility of a buyer previously using one type of machinery expanding his operation and buying another type as well.
- Knowledge of area.
- Less time away from home and so more attractive to sales force.

Advantage of product allocation of sales force:
- Apparent expertise in individual product.
- Greater technical knowledge.
- Motivation from belief in quality of product.
- Cross fertilization of ideas on installation and usage between different buyers.

B2   Major problems of obtaining initial sales (assuming correct forecast that once established the brand will do well).
So: 1.   Promotion to get product accepted by trade.
     2.   Promotion to encourage consumer trial.
       Provided the evidence of the consumer panel reflects the perception of the product by consumers generally, the market should be successful once the first trial has occurred. However, high price may be an obstacle. The company must decide whether it wants to penetrate the market or skim it. This will be dependent on production capacity and standing of other brands. The assumption here is that penetration and market share will be key objectives.
       The toothpaste market is highly competitive, so heavy advertising expenditure will be required. A new brand has to break in on consumer consciousness and break down existing brand loyalties. Where other

brands are already being advertised and promoted, the initial expenditure and effort on the new brand will have to be greater. There is always the danger of starting a promotion/advertising war where brand share is important and also the danger of raising marketing costs too high.

- Promote pack and brand name (unless linked with existing, established brands).
- Could use special introductory price offer, but may make market price conscious.
- Competitive special promotions, e.g. free toothbrush, etc., matching competitor methods, but may not be effective because the idea is not new.
- Use slogan completion in advertising to reinforce name.
- Allow quality of product to sell itself – try to keep up quality image.
- Main thrust of promotion may be at retailer/wholesaler level to persuade trade to stock it – high mark-up.
- Special offers.
- Support by using major advertising campaign at consumer level so ensuring good sales.

B3   Demand for musical instruments is likely to fall during a recession. Given high stock levels at the moment, it is in Hamelin's interests to shift them quickly. There are limited opportunities in this market but price cuts may have some effect. Free music or teach-yourself courses might create some demand.

Probably the most effective way of stimulating sales is by offering credit facilities – credit cards, hire purchase or free credit terms for large purchases. This becomes increasingly important for luxuries and consumer durables as recession hits incomes.

B4   This short case looks at the importance of distribution and organization of sales in determining the success of a company. It also shows how important they are in influencing the tactics of a company.

a.   The new competitor's approach to the market is very different from Barston's. Their segment covers large purchasers such as multiples whose sales are organized with buying offices rather than individual outlets. The implication is that this firm does not have several manufacturing plants but can distribute from a few factories. To be able to do this and to avoid repeated distribution trips, packaging plays an important part in extending the shelf life of the product. This packaging is more expensive than that used by Barston Ltd but the new firm gains other advantages in terms of economies of scale in production. It also gives limited but greater flexibility in production and allows for preparation for any seasonal peaks that may occur.

By providing a longer shelf life, the new firm can use large wholesalers who will not feel threatened by the company going

BUSINESS STUDIES

ACCEPTABLE REPORT FORMAT

The following items will be credited if they

are included in a report prepared by a

candidate during the examination.

- Title

- Sub-sections/sub-headings

- Name of author (at end of report ONLY)

- Date (at end of report ONLY)

- Introduction

- Conclusion/Recommendation(s)

directly to retailers and bypassing the wholesaler. This may help distribution and act as a threat to Barston. The small orders that Barston deals with are costly in terms of the sales force's effort.

Thus the combination of lower production and distribution costs means that the new company can remain profitable whilst using more expensive packaging material and providing the same high mark-ups to retailers that Barston gives.

b. There is a temptation to suggest that Barston should mimic the new firm's approach to the market. However, their strength lies in different areas and they may not want to close down their manufacturing plants because the costs associated with such a policy might mean that they could not invest sufficiently to match the cost benefits gained by the competitor. Given that the competitor has broken into the larger markets it would be more difficult for Barston to get in.

Thus, Barston should probably remain in its current market, developing new meat products to complement its range. Its emphasis should be on the freshness of its products and the greater flexibility it has to react to changes in the market, so making the most of new opportunities. Constant attention to the product and improvements to it may enable it to move upmarket and develop a more exclusive 'delicatessen/health' image and product. It is worth improving packaging to match that of competitors since the quality of the product will be enhanced.

9

Pricing

Introduction

Pricing is an essential part of the mix. Since total sales revenue is generated by the number of units sold multiplied by the unit price, the setting of the price level is extremely important. It is surprising how many companies seem to set their prices in an *ad hoc* way, or neglect the market conditions and try to cover costs with some mark-up for profit. Choosing the right price depends on a mass of factors including the objectives of the firm in terms of profit and volume of sales, the competitive environment, the image that the product has (hence the basic distinction between cheap and cheerful and quality/high price), etc.

As with all the marketing area, there are plenty of examples to look at. It is instructive to discuss the price of products with a group and find out whether they think the products are 'good value'. People's perception of good value varies enormously but they frequently use price as an indication of quality. Thus price is an important part of the communication with the customer.

Main teaching points

9.2   *The meaning of price*
      Consumers need to be clear about what they are comparing when they look at the prices of different products. Petrol may be cheaper at a garage fifteen miles away but the cost of going there to fill up the car may be more than the difference in price charged by the local garage. Nevertheless, price is not the only factor affecting a purchase decision.

9.3   *Price in the economic sense*
      The idea of supply and demand and the market mechanism is an essential basis for what follows in the chapter. It is worth bringing out the drawbacks of the theory in that lack of information and irrational behaviour by consumers make the market mechanism imperfect at best.

9.4   *Pricing and the market environment*
      This section takes the market mechanism and adds other factors influencing price and pricing decisions.

9.5   *Pricing and objectives*

Since price is one of the factors affecting the volume of sales, market share, market growth, profits and other objectives (image, etc.) will affect the price set by the firm. Objectives should be seen long term as well as short term. Low prices and profits may be necessary in the short term to build up market share and leadership so that the firm can manipulate pricing decisions in the future. (The French have argued against allowing Japanese car imports because they see the Japanese building market share and then increasing prices once they have a stranglehold on a particular segment of the market – as appears to have happened in the US market for small cars.)

9.6   *Pricing strategies*

Market skimming and market penetration affect the whole life of the product and the image of the firm. A penetration policy has implications for all aspects of the mix and the objectives set out by the firm. Successful pricing strategies are usually indicated by relatively rare price changes. *Apricot Computers* went through a phase of rapidly changing prices to such an extent that dealers did not know what to charge. This indicated a lack of clarity about what the market would bear and how the costs of the machines would be covered. The consequence of this uncertainty was a reluctance to purchase by many in the market.

9.7   *Methods of pricing*

Different methods are used to match different situations for each product. Pricing in markets where there are many suppliers is usually influenced by competitor decisions. Markets served by few suppliers may be more cost based. No company can afford to ignore either costs or the market for long and pricing is often an amalgam of the two approaches. The various methods described in this section cover both sides: break-even is a good way to bring costs and revenues together.

9.8   *Psychological price*

Price tells consumers about a product in terms of their perception of quality and value. Pricing a product outside the range of expectations will deter purchasers unless there is an explanation given. Providing that explanation is expensive. Some firms deliberately price outside the 'normal' range such as *Stella Artois* which makes a point of pricing high and promotes on this basis: 'reassuringly expensive', 'possibly the most expensive lager in the world'.

Guide to Exercises

B1   Before the order:

		(£)	
Sales	5,000 at £6.50	32,500	
Less direct costs	5,000 at £5	25,000	
		7,500	
Contribution to overheads		10,000	(5,000 × £2)
	Loss	(2,500)	

New order:		
Sales	3,000 at £6	18,000
Less direct costs	3,000 at £5	15,000
Contribution		3,000

Thus, with the new order, the loss of £2,500 is converted to a profit of £500. They should take the order because they have spare capacity and overheads remain constant unless:

- Own brand sales will reduce company's own sales.
- A better order is available.
- The capacity could be used for a different product.
- The company expects its own sales to rise and 'own-brand' competition will damage the product's image.

B2   a.   Break-even output.
Let x = number of chairs sold.
Price to Hillside Enterprises = £12.50 (50% of £25 is distributor margin).
Therefore at break even:

$$12.5x \quad = \quad 8.5x + £7,000$$

Therefore x = 1,750 chairs
(This can also be shown graphically.)

b.   Profit on 1,800 chairs.

Contribution: $(12.5 - 8.5) \times 1800 \quad = \quad £7,200$
Therefore profit = £7,200 − £7,000 = £200

c.   Profit of £3,000.

Let output $\quad = \quad x$
Therefore £3,000 $\quad = \quad 12.5x - (8.5x + £7,000)$
Therefore $\quad 4x \quad = \quad$ 10,000 chairs
$\qquad\qquad x \quad = \quad$ 2,500 chairs

d.   Profit on 3,500 chairs.

Sales revenue	$3,500 \times £11$	=	£38,500
Direct costs	$3,500 \times £8.50$	=	£29,750
Contribution		=	£8,750
Fixed overhead		=	£7,000
Therefore profit		=	£1,750

This is a better profit than on 1,800 chairs (equivalent to sales of 2,213 chairs at £25). Whether the company will reduce prices is dependent on their view of the strength of the market. If successful and 3,000 chairs are sold at £25 the company will make £5,000 profit. So there is a need to balance risk and return.

B3   *Brecon Ltd*

Note: the objective of this case is to see if students can apply some of the basic principles of pricing to a specific situation. Since we are trying to apply principles it may be well worth getting them to list the principles first, then to see how many are applicable in this case and finally what their particular significance is. The situation is made somewhat easier as the question asks for the decision to be based on numerate and non-numerate material and this allows the student a two-pronged attack. It is worth noting the weight given to either side, since costing and market information make up only two of a possible six determinants of price.

Basic principles:

1.   Consumer demand ⟶ market { size / condition

2.   Costs of production
3.   Competitors
4.   Other parts of mix

5.   Time factor { short-term / long-term

6.   Environment ⟶ Government { taxes / subsidies / legislation

Apply these to case:

What information can be gathered in each of these? Classify it as case suggests into numerate and non-numerate.

Numerate:

1.   *Demand-market*
   - Total size forecast (800,000).
   - Share forecast (25% assuming 75p price).
   - Share down to 75/100,000 units if price £1.
   - Revenue – £1 per unit for 75p per unit.

2. *Costs*
   - Some useful costing information given and students should put this in the form of a marginal costing table to examine the financial viability of the lines.
   - How up-to-date is this information?

Marginal costing statement (cost per unit)

	75,000		100,000	200,000 units
Sales revenue	£1.00		£1.00	75p
Costs				
Direct: Labour	28p		26p	16p
Machines	17p		17p	14p
Spoilage	5p		6p	8p
Variable overheads	16p		15p	18p
Marginal cost	66p	66p	64p	64p	56p	56p
Contribution factor		34p	36p	19p
Fixed overheads		33p	32p	28p
(50% factor costs)		1p	4p	-9p

Non-numerate:
1. *Market*: We are not told much about the market – whether it is expanding – static – contracting; assumptions necessary – (e.g. expansion because of economies?)
2. *Costs:* There is a hint of economies of scale (no figures); there is the important point that resources cannot be *reallocated*, posing problems for the production line.
3. *Competitors:*
   - A large number of small competitors.
   - Most (if not all) working on small margins, therefore relatively precarious.
   - Gradually gnawing away at Brecon's market share.
4. *Mix:*
   - Brecon a *price* leader and therefore has a lot of power if it can maintain ground.
   - Trained sales force but not apparently working on bonus, etc.; useful if sales to be pushed.
   - Nothing on other parts of the mix.
5. *Time factor:*
   - Probably more important than at first thought because

numerate information shows that loss is being made in the short term. The question must therefore arise as to what it might do in the short term and whether or not this would be adequate for long term and allow the firm to reach its longer term objectives (whatever these are).

6.   *Environment*:
   • No specific information given therefore ignore in general terms.

Decision:

Price £1 – output 75/100,000

• Safety first policy ... (short term).
• OK if you can reach 100,000.
• Not necessarily stop price cutting or diminishing market share.
• This means you may have to return to this problem in longer term.
• Poor base for longer-term move to gain from economies of scale.
• Could lead to many long-term worries.
• That other part of mix might need changing to prevent loss of market?

Price at 75p – output 200,000

• More risk in short-term ... but long-term gain.
• Marginal loss numerically in short-term but high contribution factor and resources cannot be used elsewhere.
• Opportunity to try and end price war and loss of market share by squeezing narrow-margin competitors to the wall.
• This would clear ground for any longer-term expansion and economies (suggested).
• All this is based on Brecon achieving sales forecast – thus probably necessary to alter some other parts of the mix to do this (suggestions?); if competitors fall, change in mix might be small.

On balance, the more adventurous action seems to suggest you drop your price and go for the longer-term solution.

Note: This is a good example of a case where numerate information is only one element in the decision. Also, the lack of information on the way the market is moving, the time factor, and no clear statement of the firm's objectives make assumptions necessary and so no one solution possible.

B4   *Granham Co. Ltd*

Note: As in Brecon Ltd, the objective here is to apply some of the basic principles of pricing to a specific situation. If thought worth it, list the principles first and then see how many apply to this case and their significance. Although the questions are subdivided they still fall basically into the two subdivisions of the previous case – numerate (a and b) and non-numerate (c).

Basic principles:
Consumer demand.
Costs of production.
Competition.
Other parts of the mix.
Time factor.
Environment

} How many of these apply to the case?

Apply these to case:
Subdivide information into numerate and non-numerate.
Numerate:
Demand-market: no information given.
Costs: some useful costing information, and you are asked to look at two sets of figures:

- That available when the order arrived.
- That available after additional figures have been requested.

To see the full value of these it is best to set out as marginal costing statements so that information for decision-making can be easily assimilated (excellent if the student realizes this).

Marginal costing statement (cost per unit)

Table I	(£)	(£)	Table II	(£)	(£)
Sales revenue		640	Sales revenue		640
Costs:			Costs:		
Direct:			Direct:		
Labour	150		Labour	157.50	
Materials	175		Materials	183.75	
Variable overheads			Variable overheads		
Existing	90		Existing	96	
Freight & imports	150★		Freight & imports	150	
Marginal cost	565	565	Marginal cost	587.25	587.25
contribution		75	contribution		52.75
Fixed overheads		120	Fixed overheads		144.00
Loss		(45)	Loss		(91.25)

$$★\left(\frac{30,000}{200}\right)$$

Note: There is little or no numerate information on any of the other principles involved in determining price.

Non-numerate:

Market-demand: little, other than it was the leading supplier therefore in strong position, the home market was reaching saturation point and there was a desire to look for other markets and even export seemed a possibility.

(*Note*: no specific objectives given.)

Costs: realization that these might be tight but not too much worry because of the obvious profitability in the home market.

Competitors: apparently not many as Granham was said to be in strong position and not much said about competition.

Mix: nothing of significance here.

Environment: important because of:

- Possible changes in exporting policy.
- Changes in freight charges beyond the firm's control.
- Longer term problems of the currency/time and certainty of payment if exchange rates fluctuate.

  Time: important because costing information suggests a loss. While a firm may feel this justified in the short run, what about the longer term?

Decision:

To accept order

- Market indicates yes even though there are no specific objectives: if it is refused and this is their only product, firm could be in trouble.
- Cost information indicates loss on both tables but reasonable contribution in each case and also profit of home market. Good short-term position to break into market - but for how long?
- Cost information suggests firm has the capacity to cope in short run as there are no substantial rises (except freight/imports/inflation); we must assume the firm has no better offers at present.
- Marketing costs do not appear prohibitive in short run but what of long term and would they meet company objectives (whatever they are)?

To reject order

- Market may indicate an opportunity but it also indicates many long-term problems that could turn firm away.
- Setting up of marketing facilities to exploit long term.
- Dealing in foreign market, of which there is little knowledge.
- Taking into consideration all the environmental factors (listed above).
- Costs indicate a short-term decision is sound but this situation could not prevail for long because of effects on home costs rising even further and so upsetting the balance even more.
- Again, although competition is at present limited, more firms may be attracted in when they see a 'foreign' firm entering the market.

A difficult decision, because there is no guarantee of success. It is a short-term gamble, with huge possible gains if the initial breakthrough can be made. It would be worth it if:

- The firm has no better offers in the same time period.
- The alternative to such expansions is stagnation.
- The money can be recouped elsewhere, *if* a loss is made.

B5   Smiths are manufacturers of industrial plastic (not of baths sold to the consumer or building trade). They have produced a product that has distinct advantages over the competition:

- Non-scratch.
- Strength.
- Good range of colours.
- Non-fade colours.
- Same costs as other manufacturers.

Pricing is part of the mix and will depend on the decision taken by the firm as to what market share the company wants, and whether there are learning/experience curve effects that will lose the cost advantage if it does not go for the volume necessary to match other established bath producers.

Other factors that will influence the decision will be the finance it has available to build the production facility, and the company's view as to its marketing and production experience relevant to this market.

Production expertise may be there given that the company is used to making industrial products in (presumably) large volumes. However, it is outside the main business of the company and it might be an option to license production to another major bath manufacturer leaving the marketing to them as well.

Given the general lack of experience, the company should probably go for a skimming policy. The product is better than competitors' models and a premium price could easily be charged. The advantage of skimming is that it requires lower investment in both marketing and production so that the financial risk is lower.

Distribution, promotion and advertising would be limited and the expertise of specialist retail outlets and wholesalers could be used. Pricing the product high means that margins for dealers could be good, so encouraging them to sell the product. There would be funding for advertising in specialist trade publications and consumer magazines with high-income readership profiles. Profit margins will be high so enabling a rapid return on investment and additional funding for expansion as the company gains experience of the market and production problems.

The new plastic will be protected from copying by other companies through patents. However, if the company goes for a large market share there will be an incentive for competitors to develop a new product quickly. This will be less of a problem if Smiths go for a small market niche.

After the launch of the products, Smiths can start to look at another range that would go for the mass market at a lower price for future expansion.

B6 The apple juice made by Appletree came about as a result of the search for ways to use apples from the orchard business that were too small for sale as apples. The apples are distinctive and the juice is of unique taste and quality.

a. Appletree sold to supermarket chains because:
  • They had no experience of marketing such a product.
  • Initial effort to break into the production side.
  • Supermarkets were guaranteed markets that would take all that Appletree produced.
  • Earlier in the product life cycle, before the market had become mature, margins were higher (?) so giving a reasonable return.
  • Probably the best solution at the time given the constraints on the firm – drawback that it did not give distinctiveness and premium pricing that the product could have commanded.

b. The problems that Appletree was facing were:
  • Heavy stockholding costs.
  • Need for more capacity to meet higher demand.
  • Mature market meant that margins were squeezed as price competition increased.
  • Low return on investment and insufficient funds to finance expansion.
  • Danger that they would be squeezed out of the market by larger producers.

c. Changes to marketing and pricing strategy:
  • Need to re-position the product which requires re-think of whole marketing strategy.
  • Leave the supermarket outlets and go for health shops and up-market outlets.
  • Re-package and promote 'new' product.
  • Price the product higher in line with the new image of a specialist, luxury product.
  • See whether it is possible to negotiate terms that lead to faster- or pre-payment.
  • Perhaps seek agreement with other fruit juice bottlers on distribution and promotion.
  • Try to find other producers who need bottling capacity to enable use through the year and not just in the autumn/early part of the year.

B7   *'All the Talents' Clothing Ltd*

 a (i) Restriction of trade achieved through tariffs or quotas. This would reduce foreign competition and make it slightly easier for ATT to sell products in the UK, although ATT's main market is at the top end where imports are the least significant.

   Sales may be affected more by reflating the economy and raising spending.

  (ii) Quantity demanded will change by four times the percentage change in price.

   Reasonably consistent from day to day.

   Linear relationship between the changes.

   Reasonable assumption that everything else is held constant: advertising costs; competitors' prices; competitors' actions; etc.

  (iii) Variable costs rise over the whole range because of increases in unit labour costs. This increase is due to:

   1. Overtime bonus.

   2. Shiftwork bonus.

   Additionally, there is a rise over the latter part of the range due to higher maintenance costs. These arise because of:

   1. Shortage of time to maintain equipment if it is working for longer hours (maintenance will be at unsocial hours' rate).

   2. Heavier and more continuous use means that breakdowns are more likely to occur. Wear will be greater.

  (iv) Cost of shirts £9.00 each.

   This assumes that fixed cost will be spread across 100,000 shirts. If the number of shirts produced is higher then fixed cost per unit will be lower and therefore total unit cost is lower. The increase in volume would have to be fairly large for the unit cost to fall below £7.00 (revenue = 50% of retail price). Mr Fox is keen to break into the mid-price range.

 b. If the price is cut by 30% (£20 − £14), then sales should increase by 30 × 4 = 120%.

  New sales level is 100,000 + (100,000 × 120/100) = 220,000

Cost of 220,000 shirts

		(£)	(£)
Materials	220,000 × 1.20		264,000
Labour	120,000 × 1.50		180,000
	40,000 × 2.00		80,000
	60,000 × 2.40		144,000
Maintenance	160,000 × 0.30		48,000
	60,000 × 0.40		24,000
Fixed costs			600,000
Total costs			1,340,000
Revenue	220,000 at £7.00		1,540,000
Profit			200,000

Alternatively and more rapidly by contribution:

	(£)
120,000 at £4.00	480,000
40,000 at £3.50	140,000
60,000 at £3.00	180,000
Contribution to fixed costs + profit	800,000
Less fixed costs	600,000
Profit	200,000
Tax @ 30%	60,000
Profit after tax	140,000
Dividend (at last year's rate)	60,000
Retained profit	80,000

c. The case states that the middle sector is more competitive and in view of this and the different distribution channels operating, several changes are necessary :

1. The company will need to change its advertising policy and promote more into the market to gain both distribution and sales.

2. There will need to be a review of the credit policy. More account will have to be taken of competitor credit terms and an analysis of how responsive sales are to credit. As more outlets and links in the distribution channel are used, so the length of payment time may increase.

3. The policy of waiting for buyers to come to the firm will have to change. Both selling through assistance at outlet level and advertising will be necessary to break into the new outlets and to establish the new position of the company and its products.

4. A larger sales force is necessary both to cover a wider area and deal with a higher volume of sales, and to assist with the new outlets in establishing the firm.

5. In the early days the firm may need to undercut competitors to achieve sufficient market penetration to justify the change to the mid-range in the market. The danger with this is that it may affect the image of the top end of the market.

6. The question of the concept of the product. Can the firm still rely on the 'quality' image? This could be a major selling point if a more skimming type policy were introduced. The problem with such an approach would be that volume might not be sufficient to be profitable in spite of higher margins than competitors in this range. Is there a midpoint between the two 'top' categories and a possible niche for ATT? Advertising and image creation will be crucial in developing the correct fit with the market.

Given the lower experience of marketing in this higher volume part of the market, ATT will be dependent on the input from the distribution channel. Information gathering will need to be improved since the direct contact with outlets will be less. Since the sector is more competitive, design changes and monitoring of trends in the market will be essential.

Although not asked for, one of the major factors will be the ability of ATT to produce the lower priced products efficiently and the company's production capacity constraint. They have just spent £0.5 m. on a custom-built production line that may not be usable for the cheaper products. Are the skills of the employees right for the different production?

d.(i)1. Revenue fell by £41,000 but the price per shirt rose by 20p. Sales volume fell by 7000 shirts.

Calculation:

Gain	20p × 110,000	£22,000
Loss	7,000 × £9.00	(£63,000)
Reduction in revenue		£41,000

or:

Gain	20p × 103,000	£20,600
Loss	7,000 × £8.80	(£61,600)
		£41,000

2. Variable costs were up by 18p per shirt. Fewer were sold but each cost more.

Gain	£2.60 × 7,000	£18,200
Loss	18p × 103,000	(£18,540)
		£340

3. Fixed costs were up by £15,920.

Total therefore £41,000 + £340 + £15,920 = £57,260

Relevant economic business factors might include:

- Stagnant market.
- Effect of higher price reducing demand (elasticity).
- Sharply increased materials costs.
- Under-used labour.

(ii). It appears that there has been little communication in either setting the budget or in giving those affected by it the information. Neither production nor marketing saw the whole budget and the relationship between the various items; hence profit was not taken into account.

1.   Origin of budget: no consideration of sales information; unrealistic labour costs.

2.   Commitment/motivation of those responsible. They need to be involved in the setting of the budget and clearly responsible for achieving the targets.

3.   Publish a fuller range of targets; specific ones can give a misleading picture, as in the case here with apparent success.

4.   Lack of feedback during the year. There should be regular information – preferably in the form of variances from the budget so that corrective action can be taken. The idea of management by exception.

5.   Flexible budgets could be used to allow for volume changes, so highlighting price/efficiency changes and pointing to the necessary corrective action.

e.   Assume that the skilled worker earns £200 per week. Redundancy money would be £4000.

Being unemployed would probably mean competing with others who have the same skill locally and therefore the chances of further employment may be limited. The employees will want the firm to continue, and given that it is profitable, they will feel badly let down if it closes. It would also not fit with the 'family tradition'.

The merger option will create concern because of the uncertainty surrounding the change. Although it will provide employment, there would be no guarantee as to how long it would last or how the job content would change. If the work methods are old-fashioned, changes to gain greater profitability are likely. New work practices would lead to concern that the employee might not have the skills although this could be overcome through retraining. The merging company might close the operation down or move it to their other plant (asset stripping?). A large company might not have as good labour relations and be seen as much more impersonal.

The co-operative idea could be interesting although presumably Mr George would like a similar price to what he would have received had he sold the company. If a 10% yield is required and profits after tax are £70,000, the price for the firm would be £700,000 (Net asset valuation: £798,000). From the point of view of the employee, the ownership would involve expenditure to buy into the co-operative and he might not like to be so heavily involved. There is a danger of loss of management expertise.

10

Production

Introduction

Production covers the manufacture of goods or the provision of services. Manufacturing is the main source of production theory but, increasingly, the principles of manufacturing, the division of labour, and the efficiency improvements resulting from specialization, are being applied to the provision of services. Information technology and the use of computers have hastened this change with control systems and information handling being as relevant for service industries as for the manufacturing sector.

It can be instructive to take a group to a manufacturing plant to see production in operation. To get the most out of such a visit, it is important to provide an introductory session beforehand, explaining the method being used to make products or components and how it works. Students will then be aware of the layout and the sort of materials handling that is used. Look at the way the production system influences the marketing of the product (e.g. a butter-packing factory may need to alter prices to ensure that sales meet the output) and help to determine the type of new products that can be introduced. Stock management will seem much more relevant after students have seen the problems of a real manufacturing facility.

Main teaching points

10.2 Types of production

Production systems range in a continuous way from job to process flow. Three categories, job, batch and flow, are explained in this section and students should understand their implications in terms of set-up time, layout and type of equipment required, skill levels, etc. At the flow end of the production spectrum, much of the equipment and skills are dedicated to the process.

Robots and computer controlled production lines are giving greater facility to production systems since a greater variety of jobs can be carried out. Similarly, for many manufacturing processes which used to be carried out in huge production lines, it is now possible to operate in smaller units because of the flexibility computers have given managers. This has implications for motivation and the use of the work force.

10.4 Sub-contracting production or services

Most students will be familiar with the idea of sub-contracting (e.g. in building work) if not the name. Advantages and disadvantages should be examined. There is increasing use of sub-contractors as businesses become more specialized. Many management buy-outs have meant that small, specialist divisions have been spun off major organizations who continue to use their services on a sub-contracting basis. Much of Japanese industry is based on this principle.

10.5 Stocks

The numerate aspects of stock control are examined in *Quantitative decision making* (in this series) but here the purpose of holding stock is seen as part of the production process. Opportunity cost can be brought in here as well as the financial consequences of holding stock. (During the miners' strike in the early eighties, the CEGB's stock of coal cost in excess of £300 m. purely in holding costs – financial and others.)

10.6 Materials handling

Just-in-time systems have been heralded as the solution to stock problems for industry. As with all panaceas, that is an overstatement and JIT can only be used in certain types of manufacturing facility. It requires close cooperation with suppliers, and for a full system, with customers as well. However, the principle of reducing stock levels and the number of times stock is handled holds good since both cost companies a great deal. Lower stock levels also reduce the risk of obsolescence and cut the assets tied up in warehousing, etc.

Guide to Exercises

B1   The question requires the synchronization of equipment outputs and inputs to allow flow production. For both parts, some equipment lies idle.

a.   *Widgets*: flow production *is* possible, at 1200/hour, i.e. 4 × Puncher, 3 × Gruncher and 2 × Thumper.

b.   *Squidgets:* flow production would only be possible at 1500/hour, requiring 15 × Puncher, 10 × Gruncher and 3 × Thumper. Thus there is insufficient plant for flow production.

B2	Product	Flow/batch	Line runs at	Line runs for
	1	F	400/hr	10 hrs
	2	B	-	-
	3	F	600/hr	10 hrs
	4	F	400/hr	5 hrs
	5	B	-	-
	6	F	500/hr	10 hrs

B3   a.

Midpoint of each group (x)	Frequency (f)	(f × x)
3	4	12
8	10	80
13	50	650
18	15	270
23	20	460
28	1	28
	$\Sigma f = 100$	$\Sigma fx = 1500$

(i) Modal group = 11 – 15 (most frequently occurring group)

$$\text{Mean} = \frac{\Sigma fx}{\Sigma f} = \frac{1500}{100} = 15$$

Median = mid-value = average of 50th and 51st week = 13
but if the distribution is regular through the group, the 50th is 36
(50–14) through the 50 in that group and the 51st is 37 through the
50 in the group, so:

$$\text{Median} = \frac{\dfrac{36}{50} \times 5^1 + \dfrac{37}{50} \times 5^1}{2} = 3.65 \ (+ 11^2) = 14 \text{ to nearest whole number}$$

^{1}5 is the interval of the group
^{2}11 is the start of this group

(ii) The mean is the most appropriate measure of central tendency since all values are taken into account.

The mode is used when we are interested only in the most commonly occurring value – it ignores the outside values and may not be near the centre of the distribution (*cf.* skewed distribution). Limited production that will cover only the largest single part of the market would provide the use for the mode.

The median would be used when there are outlying values that seriously distort the mean value, e.g. if in one of the hundred weeks examined in this question, sales were 50 units.

b. (i) Assume that the distribution of sales within the groups is even and that the sales pattern is independent of the stock levels. Also, assume that if there is no stock, the customer will not wait until there is sufficient. If there is no stock, the sale is lost to a competitor.

If the stock level falls to 24 at the beginning of each week:

in each 100-week period: 4 sales would be lost once (28 ➤ 24)
1 sale would be lost 4 times (25 ➤ 24)
Total: 8 sales in 2 years
4 sales/year = loss in contribution of
4 × £50 = £200

(ii)   Cost per unit of stock is £2 per week = £100 per year.
Thus: if stock level rose from 24 to 25 the additional cost would be
£100; lost sales would be 3 in two years = 1.5 per year = £75.
Thus additional contribution would be £25 + £100 = £125 (£100
contribution from the 21–25 group + the £25 from the next group).

At a stock level of 26 the additional contribution would be £25
against an additional cost of £100 for stock holding.

Thus optimum stock level would be 25 units.

(iii)   Consequences of running out of stock: loss of goodwill which
might lead to loss of future orders and also a loss of sales on other
lines as the customer changes to a different outlet.

Some of the uncertainty could be reduced through more frequent
deliveries of smaller levels of stock and prediction of future sales
levels if the pattern is seasonal or subject to clear peaks and troughs.

B4   a.

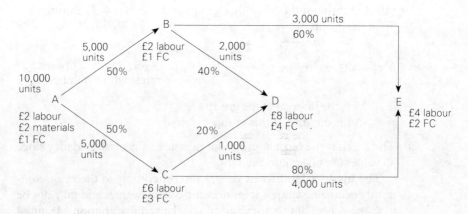

Fig 10.1

b. Dept:	Units	Cost		Total	
A	10,000 × £4	=	£40,000	Direct costs
	10,000 × £1	=	£10,000	Fixed costs
B	5,000 × £2	=	£10,000	Direct costs
	5,000 × £1	=	£5,000	Fixed costs
C	5,000 × £6	=	£30,000	Direct costs
	5,000 × £3	=	£15,000	Fixed costs
D	3,000 × £8	=	£24,000	Direct costs
	3,000 × £4	=	£12,000	Fixed costs
E	7,000 × £4	=	£28,000	Direct costs
	7,000 × £2	=	£14,000	Fixed costs

Total direct costs: £132,000
Total fixed costs: £56,000
Total costs: £188,000

Fixed costs are split 50% those incurred within department and 50% allocated from the general factory overheads of the company.

c. Products coming from D have unit costs as follows:
2,000 units via ABD: cost/unit £5 + £3 + £12 = £20
1,000 units via ACD: cost/unit £5 + £9 + £12 = £26
Total cost for 3,000 units: 2,000 × £20 + 1,000 × £26 = £66,000
                cost/unit = £22
Products coming from D have unit costs as follows:
3,000 units via ABE: cost/unit £5 + £3 + £6 = £14
4,000 units via ACD: cost/unit £5 + £9 + £6 = £20
Total cost for 7,000 units: 3,000 × £14 + 4,000 × £20 = £122,000
                cost/unit = £17.43

d. Purchase of output at A for £5.20: cost to Garplan £5.00 so profit of £0.20 per unit.
    Sell back to Garplan at £13 so reducing cost by £1.00/unit. Total apparent saving: £1.20 per unit.
    If department C were closed 50% of the overheads would no longer be incurred. However, 50% of fixed costs would still have to be covered by the rest of the organization. Thus the overhead of £1.50/unit would have to be paid, so resulting in a loss of 30p/unit if the offer from the other firm was taken up.

e. Sub-contracting the work of department C, if the price charged to Garplan were below £13.70/unit, it might look attractive financially. The drawback would be that Garplan would be at the mercy of the sub-contractor for 50% of its output. It might also happen that the sub-contractor would try to break into the market with a product similar to Garplan's.
    If department C were closed, the sub-contractor might then put prices up and so increase the overall costs for Garplan. Unexpected orders might not receive the priority that Garplan would give because the sub-contractor might not have the scheduling flexibility required. Garplan would also lose control over quality.

B5 a.

	Monday	Tuesday	Wednesday	Thursday	Friday
Opening stock:	3,000	4,000	5,500	6,000	4,000
Less: sales:	1,000	1,000	1,500	4,000	3,000
Add: production:	2,000	2,500	2,000	2,000	2,000
Closing stock:	4,000	5,500	6,000	4,000	3,000

b.

Overtime worked on:	Daily closing stocks on:				
	Monday	*Tuesday*	*Wednesday*	*Thursday*	*Friday*
Monday	4,500	5,500	6,000	4,000	3,000
Tuesday	4,000	5,500	6,000	4,000	3,000
Wednesday	4,000	5,000	6,000	4,000	3,000
Thursday	4,000	5,000	5,500	4,000	3,000
Friday	4,000	5,000	5,500	3,500	3,000

Thus Thursday or Friday would be the best days to avoid high closing stocks. Thursday gives the least variation.

c.

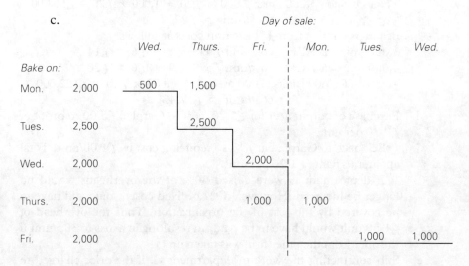

Fig 10.2

Hence only 1,000 pies are sold on the day after manufacture, so 9,500 (90.5%) are two or more days old. (Some sold on Wednesday were made the previous Friday .... which might alter buying habits somewhat!)

11

Work study and quality control

Introduction

Both work study and quality control are about improving efficiency and cost effectiveness of production. They look at achieving the most from people, machines, materials and energy. Work study considers how jobs are done and alternative ways of doing them. It includes ergonomics which examines the layout of equipment and operating controls so that employees can perform their tasks as efficiently and comfortably as possible. This is not only good for employees but also for the firm since employee performance should be enhanced. Similarly, quality control looks at the way faulty output can be avoided and so prevent defective goods and services from being sold to customers. Like work study, it is an attempt to reduce costs and waste. Poor quality control is not only expensive, it damages the reputation of companies and lowers the morale of the work force. Both aspect of 'control' are linked to value analysis, in that product design has an impact on the production process; designing quality into products is a positive part of value added.

Main teaching points

11.2 The elements of work study

There are two main aspects to work study: work measurement, which looks at how long a particular job should take and how much material/ energy it should involve; and method study which looks at the content of a job and tries to develop new and more efficient ways of doing it. Both aspects use the standard decision-making approach of objectives, information, analysis and choice. After measurement, standards for jobs or part jobs are set and employees are rated against this standard. Once standard times for different tasks have been ascertained, larger orders made up of several different jobs can be costed to produce *standard costs* (see *Accounting and Financial Decisions* by D.R. Myddelton in this series) for budgeting purposes and contract pricing. The learning curve shows the relationship between costs and cumulative output as performance improves with experience. Contracts for jobs that are price sensitive may be won through judicious estimating of the learning-curve effect.

Work study can be used to help build up a fair payment system for employees. Payment according to results should not be seen as a means of motivating employees, but rather as just reward for the work they have done. Genuine motivation remains in the content of the job and the feeling of achievement it brings.

11.3 Quality control

Quality control should be seen as an activity that goes on throughout the production process, from the quality of the raw materials the company uses to the standard of the final product. To be effective, the emphasis on quality control must come from the top and accountability for quality control must run right through the organization. Everyone should be responsible for the quality of the work they do, and reject work should be discarded as soon as it occurs.

The costs of putting defects right at a late stage in the production process or after production are high, partly because defects that are worked on subsequently represent a waste of resources and partly because repair is expensive. It disrupts production schedules and raises unit costs. As incomes have risen, so consumers have become more discerning about the quality of what they buy. The cost to the firm in terms of its reputation if faulty products reach the consumer is more difficult to identify but the damage to the firm's standing can have long term consequences in terms of sales.

Quality circles are means of involving more people in the company in improving quality. Groups get together regularly to discuss quality problems and the results of suggestions to improve the situation can be implemented in the production system. In any case, the regular communication and consultation is effective in motivating employees and improving performance.

Statistical techniques for quality control mechanisms are covered in *Quantitative decision making* (in this series).

Guide to Exercises

B1	a.	Study No.	Rating	Observed time (mins)		Basic time (mins)
		1	$\frac{110}{100}$	$\times$	2.05	= 2.26
		2	$\frac{100}{100}$	$\times$	2.10	= 2.10
		3	$\frac{110}{100}$	$\times$	2.05	= 2.26

Study No.	Rating		Observed time (mins)		Basic time (mins)
4	$\dfrac{90}{100}$	$\times$	1.90	$=$	1.71
5	$\dfrac{90}{100}$	$\times$	1.95	$=$	1.76
6	$\dfrac{100}{100}$	$\times$	2.10	$=$	2.10
7	$\dfrac{85}{100}$	$\times$	1.80	$=$	1.53
8	$\dfrac{100}{100}$	$\times$	1.70	$=$	1.70

b. The best estimate of standard time will come from the mean of the basic times in part (a) plus the 10% addition for rest time, etc.

mean basic time $=$

$$\frac{2.26+2.10+2.26+1.71+1.76+2.10+1.53+1.70}{8} = 1.93 \text{mins}$$

So standard time $= 1.93 + 10\% \times 1.93 = 2.12$ minutes

c. The range of basic times is fairly wide. For study 8 the implication is that the employee works at the normal rate but does the job very efficiently and does not waste time on unnecessary movements.

In such a case, it would be worth examining carefully the way the operator works to find out how the job practice of the particular task could be modified for the others, using the expertise of operator 8. Before a decision to do this is taken, the supervisor should examine the findings and measurements to ensure no mistake has been made. Changing work practices is often seen as threatening and should not be undertaken unless there is ample evidence that there will be significant benefits.

B2. a. The method used by Velcro for quality control before 1985 was the traditional approach taken by most firms with quality inspection points throughout the production process. Quality inspectors checked work as it came through and rejected faulty products. The inspection was effective in that faulty tape did not reach the customer. However, it was expensive since large quantities had to be scrapped. Insufficient information passed from the inspectors to the people on the line and to the management so that nothing was done about the causes of the defective tape.

b. GM complained about the quality-control system, in spite of receiving only good quality tape, because the quality of the inputs that a company uses are crucial in determining the quality of the output. In the case of GM, failure of the tape would reflect badly on GM and damage their reputation.

Although the product was delivered on time and in good quality, GM considered that the 5-8% reject rate by Velcro was too high. It meant that the production costs of Velcro were higher than they needed to be and that there was poor value added in the factory (working on defective tape which would later be scrapped). That meant that capacity was being used more fully than it needed to be and that the likelihood of delivery failure was greater. As GM moved more towards a just-in-time system, failure on delivery was too great a risk to take when it could relatively easily be put right with the correct quality-control measures. Quality-control improvement was in the interests of Velcro if they were to remain cost competitive.

c. Velcro improved quality control significantly (50% in the first year and a further 45% in the next) while reducing the number of quality-control inspectors. The approach was altered from having inspectors checking other people's work (so reducing the pressure on them to get it right, since someone else would pick up any faults) to making employees responsible for their own quality. They were encouraged to reject material as soon as a fault was found. Further, regular meetings were set up so that quality problems could be examined. This meant that information passed from those who were working on the line and could see the problems more easily to those who had the job of designing the production line. Improvements recommended by the line employees improved the productivity of the plant as well as the quality of the output. The employees, in turn, were better motivated.

d. The President of the company's presence at the quality meetings was important in showing the whole company that quality was a priority for the company and for the top management. Introducing a new procedure for quality control and instilling new attitudes in the workforce is far easier and more effective if the chief executive is involved, and seen to be involved. It means that he has a better understanding of the problems involved. Given the effect on the output of the company, it also seems as if it should have had the priority it was given (and represents good use of the chief executive's time).

The problem was highlighted by GM, a major customer of the company, with the threat of loss of the GM business if Velcro's quality management was not improved. Also, in response to strong competition earlier in the decade on the products Velcro was making, the company had decided to go 'up-market' where quality was crucial for sales. Thus the chief executive was right to take such an active role as the whole competitive position, marketing strategy and production principles were under threat. Quality control should involve everyone in the organization and the best way to ensure that it does is for the chief executive and senior management to become heavily committed to it.

12

Control and review

Introduction

The final stage of any decision-making process should be a comparison between what actually happens and what was expected at the start. This is the control and review stage. Budgets lay down the detailed working for companies; control and review show where things have gone better or worse than expected and direct action to solve problems and build on strengths. The results of new initiatives, e.g. new distribution channels or cost cutting production systems, are compared with targets; sales revenue and costs (hence profit) are analysed against budgets which need to reflect changing circumstances to determine new objectives.

At the end of the chapter, section D in the Work section has two major case studies covering aspects of the whole marketing and production course.

Main teaching points

12.2 The need for budgets

Companies need to plan for the future, setting targets on the basis of overall objectives for departments to reach. Budgets cover market volumes, prices, production output, costs, manpower requirements and finance. The setting of budgets forces different departments to communicate with each other and make the most of scarce resources. Planning avoids waste.

12.3 Problems associated with the marketing budget

The market environment is changing all the time. Production budgets have less variable links between inputs and outputs, but marketing suffers from the rapid impact of changes in competitors' actions, e.g. an advertising campaign or price discounting. There is a lack of certainty about the impact of many marketing decisions, e.g. advertising to sales. Some have impacts short term while others have a much longer drawn out effect. Stopping production has an instant result: no more goods produced; stopping a promotion campaign may have little immediate effect but longer term sales may suffer. Forecasting the outcome of decisions is difficult.

12.4 Types of budget

Emphasise the variety of budgets used in business: quality, scrap, product performance, sales volume, contribution, etc.

12.6 The use of the budget for control

Develop the idea of variance analysis (covered in detail in *Accounting and financial decisions* by D.R. Myddelton in this series) as a means of establishing where problems are occurring. The budget is the basis of targets against which performance can be continuously reviewed. Variances point the way for future decisions.

Guide to Exercises

B1   a.

	Budget	*Actual*	*Variance*
Sales: units @ £10	10,000	9,000	
Sales revenue	£100,000	£90,000	(-£10,000)
Distribution	£5,000	£4,750	£250
Advertising	£15,000	£15,000	
Sales promotion	£3,500	£3,500	
Sales personnel	£10,000	£10,000	
Departmental expenses	£3,500	£3,850	(-£350)
	£37,000 £37,000	£37,100 £37,100	(-£100) (-£100)
	£63,000	£52,900	(-£10,100)

b.   Sales could be down for a variety of reasons:
- Slump in economy.
- Improved competitor's product.
- Increased expenditure on advertising and sales promotion by competitors.
- Collapse of a major buyer.
- Change in government legislation, etc.

Departmental expenses could rise as a result of :
- General inflation.
- Increases in staff and bureaucracy, etc.

Distribution is likely to be down because less output is sold.

B2   This question looks at variances and underlines the point that a negative volume variance does not automatically imply a negative revenue variance (Region 3) or the reverse (Region 2).

Region 1

	Volume ('000s of units)			Value (£'000)		
	Budget	Actual	Variance	Budget	Actual	Variance
Product A	8	10	2	40	50	10
B	6	4	(−2)	60	40	(−20)
C	4	2	(−2)	80	40	(−40)
Total	18	16	(−2)	Total 180	130	(−50)

Region 2

	Volume ('000s of units)			Value (£'000)		
	Budget	Actual	Variance	Budget	Actual	Variance
Product A	12	16	4	60	80	20
B	16	20	4	160	200	40
C	24	20	(−4)	480	400	(−80)
Total	52	56	4	Total 700	680	(−20)

Region 3

	Volume ('000s of units)			Value (£'000)		
	Budget	Actual	Variance	Budget	Actual	Variance
Product A	14	9	(−5)	70	45	(−25)
B	8	10	2	80	100	20
C	8	10	2	160	200	40
Total	30	29	(−1)	Total 310	345	35

Possible conclusions from the figures:
- Product A, the most expensive, has fallen behind the budget in Regions 1 and 2. In Region 3, C has done well but A, the cheapest, has fallen back. This could suggest a difference in income levels between the regions, with Region 3 the most prosperous.
- Region 1 is the weakest performer in value terms – some examination of problems required here. Any of the ideas suggested in the chapter could apply.
- All the value variances are sizeable – is the budgeting satisfactory or is it a very difficult market to predict? Need to show that positive variances are as big a problem as negative ones. The answers provided by the class could broaden out into a discussion on the process of setting budgets (see also B4b.).

B3   Costs based on estimates, not actual figures. The purpose of the actual figures is to show the danger of allocated overheads on the basis of sales estimates.

a.   Expected profits:

	A	B	C
Sales revenue (£)	24,000	10,000	6,000
(Estimate) percentage of total sales	60	25	15
Overheads (£)	18,000	7,500	4,500
Direct costs (£)	2,000	1,000	1,500
Profit (£)	4,000	1,500	0
Percentage of sales	16.7	15	0

b.   The managing director's reaction is likely to be a decision to cut Product C. Both A and B achieve larger returns than 10% on sales (A:16.7%, B:15%) and we know the MD is unfavourably disposed to Product C. He now has the evidence to justify stopping manufacture of it.

c.   Product managers for A and B would be happy with the system. If overheads had been allocated on the basis of actual sales they would look like this:

	A	B	C
Sales revenue (£)	35,000	14,000	6,000
(Estimate) percentage of total sales	64	25	11
Overheads (£)	19,200	7,500	3,300
Direct costs (£)	2,917	1,400	1,500
Profit	12,883	5,100	1,200
Percentage of sales	36.8	36.4	20

and all products would be well above the 10% return target.

Product C manager can reasonably claim that allocation of overheads on the basis of expected sales is unfair. His estimate is right but both A and B have underestimated their sales and so incurred disproportionately low overheads leaving the balance for C to make up. Low budget – good performances and low costs.

Also:
- We know that C is new and it may take time to establish itself.
- C may enable the firm to break into new markets.
- As part of the range, could it be a loss leader?
- A broad range of products may be essential to persuade distributors to stock the products.

B4   a.

	Budget (£)	Actual (£)	Variance (£)	Variance (%)
Revenue	130,000	160,000	30,000	23
Total advertising costs	33,000	48,500	(–15,500)	(–47)
Comprising:				
Salaries and commission	10,000	17,000	(–7,000)	(–70)
Car expenses	6,000	7,500	(–1,500)	(–25)
Exhibitions	2,000	4,000	(– 2,000)	(–100)
Production costs	15,000	20,000	(–5,000)	(–33)

In terms of increased revenue against increased costs, the balance has improved by £14,500 (£30,000 *minus* £15,500).

However, the budget revenue figures were not included and clearly they are part of the whole picture, hence part of the aggravation for the advertising manager.

With regard to the increase in wages: wage costs were said to have risen by 15%. In reality they are up 70%.

Exhibitions were up by 100% instead of the 50% expected.

Inflation of 20% in production costs does not account for the 33% rise.

So the advertising manager's justification for the figures is unsatisfactory, and the managing director may be correct in suggesting that there is little cost control. However, changed circumstances should be reflected in the budget.

b.   For a budget to be useful as part of control it should be set in consultation with all the relevant departments.

The budget should be complete (i.e. in this case revenue as well as cost figures should be included).

Other factors, e.g. declining markets, should be taken account of, when control is involved.

Where the situation changes within the budgeting period, the budget should be altered ('flexed') to take account of this.

Regular feedback is essential so that corrective action can be taken quickly.

General case studies

D1 a. (i)   Market segmentation: splitting the market up according to certain defined sectors that have different characteristics and can thus be approached in different ways. A manufacturer can produce products specific to particular segments, altering the nature of the product by, for example, its packaging and price. Most large industries serve different segments, for example, professional/trade decorators and the DIY market. Although the basic product is similar, it is modified to suit the purpose for which it is intended. Distribution channels are different by segment.

(ii)   Diagram Y shows the relative proportion of membership by age group. The range of the age groups is not the same but presumably reflects different segments identified by the management. The single biggest group is the 16-25 year range. Taken with the 26-35 year range, these two groups cover over 50% of the total membership.

For the marketing manager, this is significant in that it determines some of the services the leisure centre should provide. The other sizeable group is the over-60s who will have different requirements of the leisure centre.

The marketing manager will want to find out whether these groups spend much in the various facilities and what usage they make of them. The information does not provide evidence by usage or time of usage which could be used to target the facilities more closely.

(iii) Another form of segmentation could be by facility type – it may be more important than age and would be easy to research by ticket receipts and membership questionnaires.

Alternatively, income groups may be important to determine how much will be spent and hence the sales income for the centre. Suiting the particular market segments should increase usage. The management must be clear about its objectives for the centre and how it fits into Pringles PLC's overall objectives for profit and market share.

In each case, research will be used to improve the fit between the services and facilities that the centre provides and the demands of the members and other users.

b. Use of the centre is very seasonal since it is situated at an east coast resort where the population will vary with holidays. It is not surprising that the usage of the centre is higher in the summer and particularly in the peak month of August. Member use is fairly constant throughout the year, as is that by local residents.

(i) Market research: the company could find out what might encourage use in other months; e.g. size of conference market, number of conferences in the area.

Other factors to consider could be:
- Other similar facilities in the area.
- Extent of non-member/resident pass market in the area.
- Opportunities for switching resident passes to membership.
- Demand for special interest use of facilities, e.g. local squash club.
- Effect of price and income on demand.

(ii) Pricing: seasonal pricing, charging non-member/non-resident higher prices in the summer.
- Discounting in the off-peak season.
- Differential pricing for membership in different age groups (e.g. children and pensioners). It may be possible to build up pensioner membership.
- Hall and meeting rooms hire charges could be looked at. Differential pricing for business and personal use.
- Marginal cost pricing for off-peak use.

(iii) Suitable methods of promotion:
- Advertising locally to keep the centre in the public eye during the off-peak months.
- Advertising in business conference magazines to attract this part of the market.
- Run events to attract locals and so show them the other benefits of membership.
- Develop winter season membership.
- Promote publicity in local hotels, estate agencies, waiting rooms, etc.
- Price discounting on certain days.
- 'Happy hour' at the bars, etc. to get customers into the centre.

(iv) Changes to the product: the marketing emphasis will depend on the capacity of the centre. Assuming that it is fair in the summer the product changes should respond to needs at other times of the year.
- Training sessions for swimming/squash, etc.
- Conference facilities including secretarial, etc.
- Links with local schools for LEA paid use of the facilities.
- 'Keep-fit', squash, swimming clubs.
- Film club using the hall.

- Running parties and discos during the winter, so building up local nature of the facility as a social centre.

c.   (i)   A sales budget would show volume of use and price to generate revenue estimates for the various facilities and for membership fees. It would also cover promotion costs, advertising, etc.

The purpose would be to set targets against which performance could be judged (variance analysis) and to identify which areas need particular attention.

Taken with the costs of running the centre, Pringles PLC would have an estimate of the profit from the centre to put into their overall budget. It would also help the planning and running of the centre in terms of personnel requirements.

(ii)   If local income is expected to rise, the impact on the use of the centre will depend on the extent to which demand is income elastic. Rising income usually means that a greater proportion of disposable income will be spent on items like leisure. Thus the demand for the facilities should rise – income is probably more important than price in determining demand. Information would be needed on the groups that were expected to benefit from the increase in income and the services of the centre targeted towards them.

D2   *United Custards*

a.   (i)   *Price elasticity of demand*: measure of responsiveness of one variable (demand) to a change in another (price).

$$\frac{\% \, \Delta \, Q}{\% \, \Delta \, P}$$

(ii)   *Extension strategy*: development of new modified product or new market in order to retain or increase sales.

1. Development of new markets for existing products.
2. Development of new uses for existing products.
3. Increase usage of products.
4. Increase range of products.
5. Styling changes.

Instant soup mix an example of (2).

(iii)   *Quota sample*: sample whose make-up reflects the different categories in the population.

For example, in this case it should be constructed with 30% single, 10% married, 60% families: and 40% ABC, 60% C_2DE.

b.   Government measures leading to a reduction in average income provide little concrete information because it is unclear how each of the four categories will be affected. Different sectors, e.g. cafes and hotels, will be more or less price/income elastic.

	Tonnes	% of total
Cafes	75	37.5
Hotels	32	16
Schools	44	22
Office canteens	49	24.5
		100

- Drop in income likely to hit those eating out so cafe and hotel consumption likely to be down – accounts for 53.5% of sales, thus a good idea to try moving into consumer market (but business usage will remain the same).
- In addition, with more people at work 'convenience' foods likely to be in greater demand.
- Schools and canteens still produce a similar demand because their services are essential.

c. Price elasticity of demand:

$$\text{Increase in price} = \frac{98}{1400} \times 100 = 7\%$$

$$\text{Fall in demand} = \frac{20}{220} \times 100 = 9.1\%$$

$$\text{Therefore } \eta = \frac{9.1}{7} = 1.3$$

Average covers the whole range of powdered foods. Is the margin the same for chocolate, malt drinks, custard, soups, etc?

d. Contribution to fixed overhead at present level of sales:

Costs	200 × £1,000	=	£200,000
Revenue	200 × £1,498	=	£299,600
Contribution		=	£99,600

To increase sales from 200 to 250 tonnes the price must fall.
$\eta = 1.3$

$$\text{Therefore increase in volume} = \frac{50}{200} = 25\%$$

$$\eta = \frac{\%\Delta Q}{\%\Delta P} \quad \therefore \quad \frac{25\%}{1.3} = \%\Delta P$$

Therefore $\%\Delta P = 19.2\%$
Drop in price of 19.2% on £1,498 to £1,210.38.

Costs   250 × £1000   = £250,000
Revenue 250 × £1210.38   = £302,595
                                            (250 × £1210 = £302,500)
Therefore contribution   = £52,500

Therefore better to sell at 200 tonnes volume – £47,100 more contribution.

e. Sample 5,000
Required usership 20%
Therefore   pr. (user)   = 0.2 = p
                     pr. (non-user) = 0.8 = q
Mean = np = 1,000

$\sigma = \sqrt{npq} = 28.28 \approx 28$

To be 89% certain means the area under the normal curve must be 0.89 of the total.

0.89 = 0.5 left of mean + 0.39 to the right
0.39 ∝ 1.25σ

Therefore must have at least (mean) 1000 + 1.25 × 28 people using dried soups.
= 1035 people using dried soups from sample necessary for launch.

f.   Manufacturer ⟶ buying office ⟶ supermarket ⟶ customer

Wholesaler   independent retailers   customer

g. The final price is technically dependent on the distribution outlet.

16p + 20% (for supermarket) = 19.2p (19p)
16p + 5% = 16.8p + 15%   = 19.32p (19.5p)
   (wholesaler)   (retailer)

The distribution system is such that an increase in price ex-factory is compounded by margins charged through the chain, leading to a larger final increase to the consumer.

h. Branding: the market is already branded, therefore branding is important.

Advantages:
• Creates brand loyalty.
• Ease of identification (particularly on supermarket, self-service shelves).
• Link with packaging.
• Link with advertising.
• Diminishes importance of price in consumer's decision.
• Well-known brand can increase chance of acceptance of new product by consumer and trade.

Disadvantages:

- Manufacturer must guarantee consistent quality.
- Advertising necessary to promote brand.
- Failure of one product will damage all others in the brand.

i. Overheads are allocated in cost figures but in this case already incurred for 250 tonnes output.

Thus for new soup range 2p can be ignored at the moment – price could be reduced to 14p ex-factory giving competitive edge.

In the long run either the soups will lead to new overheads or the other products currently covering the overheads may cease to do so.

This approach does give flexibility for launching the new product.

j. Total available for promotion: 50 tonnes at 1p per 50 g

$$= \frac{50 \times 1000 \times 1000 \times 1p}{50 \text{ g}} = \pounds 100,000 \text{ p.a.}$$

Therefore:

- cannot use television advertising (would cover neither screening costs nor production costs). Best source probably local press, showing any special offers, etc.
- Angle advertising at young families (60% of the market) stressing flavour and nutritional value.
- Also importance of advertising within the trade (and also to consumer to show trade that a market for the product is available).